The Little Indonesian Cookbook

HEINZ VON HOLZEN

Marshall Cavendish Cuisine

The Little Indonesian Cookbook

Copyright © 2015 Marshall Cavendish International (Asia) Private Limited

Published by Marshall Cavendish Cuisine
An imprint of Marshall Cavendish International

All rights reserved

No part of this publication may be reproduced, stored in a retrieval system or transmitted, in any form or by any means, electronic, mechanical, photocopying, recording or otherwise, without the prior permission of the copyright owner. Request for permission should be addressed to the Publisher, Marshall Cavendish International (Asia) Private Limited, 1 New Industrial Road, Singapore 536196. Tel: (65) 6213 9300 Fax: (65) 6285 4871
Email: genref@sg.marshallcavendish.com Online bookstore: www.marshallcavendish.com/genref

Limits of Liability/Disclaimer of Warranty: The Author and Publisher of this book have used their best efforts in preparing this book. The Publisher makes no representation or warranties with respect to the contents of this book and is not responsible for the outcome of any recipe in this book. While the Publisher has reviewed each recipe carefully, the reader may not always achieve the results desired due to variations in ingredients, cooking temperatures and individual cooking abilities. The Publisher shall in no event be liable for any loss of profit or any other commercial damage, including but not limited to special, incidental, consequential, or other damages.

Other Marshall Cavendish Offices:
99 White Plains Road, Tarrytown NY 10591-9001, USA • Marshall Cavendish International (Thailand) Co Ltd. 253 Asoke, 12th Flr, Sukhumvit 21 Road, Klongtoey Nua, Wattana, Bangkok 10110, Thailand • Marshall Cavendish (Malaysia) Sdn Bhd, Times Subang, Lot 46, Subang Hi-Tech Industrial Park, Batu Tiga, 40000 Shah Alam, Selangor Darul Ehsan, Malaysia

Marshall Cavendish is a trademark of Times Publishing Limited

National Library Board, Singapore Cataloguing-in-Publication Data

Holzen, Heinz von, author.

The little Indonesian cookbook / Heinz von Holzen. – Singapore : Marshall Cavendish Cuisine, 2015.
pages cm
ISBN : 978-981-4561-25-9 (paperback)

1. Cooking, Indonesian. 2. Cookbooks. I. Title.

TX724.5.I5
641.59598 -- dc23   OCN900621702

Printed in Singapore by Markono Print Media Pte Ltd

Contents

Introduction *4*

Basic Recipes *7*

Rice & Soups *13*

Seafood *29*

Meat & Poultry *45*

Vegetables & Salads *67*

Light Meals & Snacks *83*

Glossary *102*

Weights & Measures *107*

Introduction

Indonesian cuisine is diverse, in part because Indonesia is composed of approximately 6000 populated islands. Many regional cuisines exist and are often based on cultural and foreign influences .

Throughout its history, Indonesia has been involved in trade due to its location and natural resources. Additionally, Indonesia's indigenous techniques and ingredients were influenced by India, the Middle East, China and Europe. Spanish and Portuguese traders brought new world produce to Indonesia even before the Dutch came to colonize most of the archipelago. The Indonesian islands of Maluku, which are famously known as the Spice Islands, also contributed to the introduction of native spices, such as cloves and nutmeg, to Indonesian and global cuisine.

Some popular Indonesian dishes such as *nasi goreng* (fried rice), *mie goreng*, (fried noodles) and *sates* (meat skewers) are ubiquitous in the country and considered as Indonesian national dishes and yet do not even originate from the country. *Nasi* and *mie goreng* originated from the Chinese while *sates* are found almost everywhere.

Sumatran cuisine, featuring curried meat and vegetables such as *gulai* and *kari* often has Middle Eastern and Indian influences, while Javanese cuisine is more indigenous. The cuisines of Eastern Indonesia are similar to Polynesian and Melanesian cuisine. Elements of Chinese cuisine can also be seen in Indonesian cuisine everywhere. Foods such as *bakmi* (noodles), *bakso* (meat or fish balls), and *lumpia* (spring rolls) have been completely assimilated.

Some popular dishes that originated in Indonesia are now common in South East Asia. Indonesian dishes such as *rendang sapi* (beef braised with coconut milk and spices) and sambals (spiced sauces) are highly favoured in Malaysia and Singapore while *tempeh*, a fermented soybean cake originated in Java has proven to be popular among South East Asians. Eaten on its own or in combination with other foods, soybeans provide an inexpensive and nutritious meal with its nourishing benefits.

As it is very common to eat with one's hand in parts of Indonesia such as Bali, West Java and West Sumatra, households or restaurants like seafood food stalls, traditional Sundanese and Minangkabau restaurants or even food stalls selling East Javanese *pecel lele* (fried catfish with sambal) and *ayam goreng* (fried chicken), *kobokan*, a bowl of tap water with a slice of lime is usually served. However, this bowl of water is used to wash one's hand before and after eating and should not be consumed. Eating with chopsticks is generally only seen in food stalls or restaurants serving Indonesian adaptations of Chinese cuisine, such as *bakmie* or *mie ayam* (chicken noodle) with *pangsit* (wonton), *mie goreng* (fried noodles) and *kwetiau goreng* (fried flat rice noodles).

With the large amount of foreign influences that has greatly impacted the style and taste of Indonesian cuisine, the food in Indonesia has become even more varied and vibrant. This book brings together some of the country's best-loved dishes, with one section detailing basic spice and stock recipes to help bring out the authentic flavours that are representative of Indonesia, and five different sections from mains to desserts that are sure to be a favourite at your dining table. From the rich and savoury *opor ayam* (chicken in spiced coconut sauce) to the delicious *sate manis* (assorted satays), this book is a celebration of Indonesia's culinary delights.

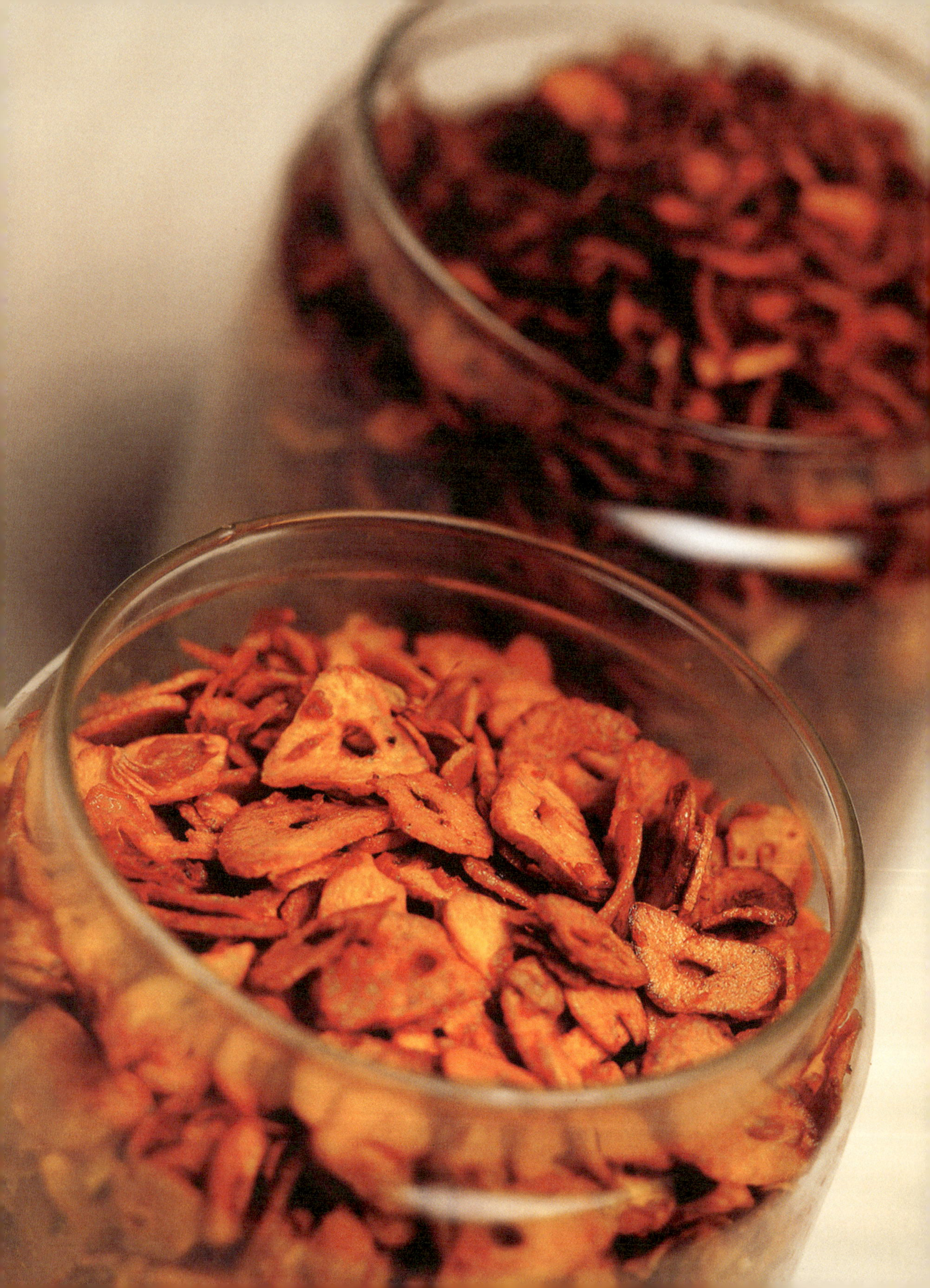

Basic Recipes

Bumbu Daging (Meat Spice Blend) 8

Bumbu Ikan (Seafood Spice Blend) 8

Bumbu Sayur (Vegetable Spice Blend) 9

Saus Pedas Tomat (Spiced Tomato Sauce) 9

Kuah Indonesia (Basic Indonesian Chicken/Beef Stock) 10

Kaldu Udang (Basic Seafood Stock) 10

Kaldu Sayur (Basic Vegetable Stock) 11

Base Sate (Peanut Sauce) 11

Bumbu Daging (Meat Spice Blend)

250 g large red chillies, halved, seeded and sliced
40 g bird's eye chillies, finely sliced
200 g shallots, peeled and sliced
50 g garlic, peeled and sliced
75 g ginger, peeled and sliced
75 g galangal *(laos)*, peeled and chopped
75 g turmeric, peeled and sliced
100 g candlenuts
1 teaspoon crushed black peppercorns
1 tablespoon crushed coriander seeds
40 g palm sugar, chopped
¾ tablespoon salt
3 *salam* leaves
150 ml coconut oil
250 ml water

1. Combine all ingredients except *salam* leaves, oil and water in a stone mortar or food processor. Grind until fine.

2. Place ground ingredients in a heavy saucepan, add remaining ingredients and cook over medium heat for approximately 1 hour or until all water is evaporated and paste takes on a golden colour.

3. Cool before using or storing in the refrigerator.

Bumbu Ikan (Seafood Spice Blend)

450 g large red chillies, seeded and sliced
20 g bird's eye chillies, finely sliced
220 g shallots, peeled and sliced
50 g garlic, peeled and sliced
175 g turmeric, peeled and sliced
100 g ginger, peeled and sliced
200 g tomatoes, grilled, peeled, halved and seeded, juice reserved
125 g candlenuts, crushed
2 tablespoons crushed coriander seeds
2 tablespoons roasted dried shrimp paste (*terasi*)
¾ tablespoon salt
4 tablespoons tamarind juice
2 kaffir lime leaves, bruised
3 *salam* leaves
2 stalks lemongrass, bruised
150 ml coconut oil
250 ml water

1. Combine all ingredients except tamarind juice, kaffir lime and *salam* leaves, lemongrass, oil and water in a stone mortar or food processor. Grind until fine.

2. Place ground ingredients in a heavy saucepan, add remaining ingredients and simmer over medium heat for approximately 1 hour or until water is evaporated and paste takes on a golden colour.

3. Cool before using or storing in the refrigerator.

Bumbu Sayur (Vegetable Spice Blend)

250 g large red chillies, halved, seeded and sliced
25 g bird's eye chillies, sliced
100 g shallots, peeled and sliced
100 g garlic, peeled and sliced
75 g galangal *(laos)*, peeled and thinly sliced
75 g fresh turmeric, peeled and sliced
50 g lesser galangal *(kencur)*, peeled and sliced
75 g ginger, peeled and sliced
100 g candlenuts
1 tablespoon crushed coriander seeds
1 teaspoon crushed white peppercorns
¾ tablespoon salt
2 *salam* leaves
2 stalks lemongrass, bruised
150 ml vegetable oil
250 ml water

1. Combine all ingredients except *salam* leaves, lemongrass, oil and water in a stone mortar or food processor. Grind until fine.

2. Place ground ingredients in a heavy saucepan, add remaining ingredients and simmer over medium heat for approximately 1 hour or until water is evaporated and paste takes on a golden colour.

3. Cool before using or storing in the refrigerator.

Saus Pedas Tomat (Spiced Tomato Sauce)

200 ml coconut oil
200 g shallots, peeled and sliced
100 g garlic, peeled and sliced
375 g large chillies, seeded and sliced
375 g bird's eye chillies, whole
50 g palm sugar, chopped
1½ tablespoons roasted dried shrimp paste *(terasi)*
750 g tomatoes, peeled and seeded
salt, to taste
1 tablespoon lime juice

1. Heat oil in a heavy saucepan, add shallots and garlic and sauté until golden. Add chillies and continue to sauté until chillies are soft.

2. Add palm sugar and shrimp paste and continue to sauté until sugar caramelizes. Add tomatoes and continue to sauté until tomatoes are soft. Set aside and cool.

3. Grind in a stone mortar or purée coarsely in food processor.

4. Season to taste with salt and lime juice.

Kuah Indonesia (Basic Indonesian Chicken/Beef Stock)

6 kg chicken carcasses or beef bones, without skin and fat, cut into 2.5-cm pieces or smaller
150 g *bumbu daging* (page 8)
2 stalks lemongrass, bruised
2 kaffir lime leaves, torn
2 large red chillies, bruised
3–5 bird's eye chillies
2 *salam* leaves
½ teaspoon coarsely crushed black peppercorns
½ teaspoon crushed coriander seeds

1. Rinse carcasses or bones until water runs clear. Transfer to a stockpot and cover with cold water. Bring to a boil over high heat to blanch carcasses or bones. Drain and discard water.

2. Rinse carcasses or bones again and return half the carcasses or bones to a larger stockpot, reserving other half for the next day.

3. Add three times as much water as carcasses or bones and bring to a boil. Lower heat and skim off any scum as it accumulates.

4. Add remaining ingredients and simmer stock over very low heat for 5–6 hours.

Kaldu Udang (Seafood Stock)

1 kg seafood shells (lobster, prawns, crabs or crayfish)
3 tablespoons coconut oil
150 g *bumbu ikan* (page 9)
2 stalks lemongrass, bruised
3 kaffir lime leaves, crushed
2 large red chillies
4–6 bird's eye chillies
2 litres water or preferably light *kuah Indonesia*

1. Clean seafood shells and discard all organs, including the gills and eyes. Chop or crush shells with a heavy knife or cleaver.

2. Heat coconut oil in a saucepan and sauté shells for 6–8 minutes until light golden brown.

3. Add *bumbu ikan*, lemongrass, kaffir lime leaves and chillies. Sauté for another 2 minutes.

4. Deglaze with 250 ml water or *kuah Indonesia* and sauté for another 2 minutes.

5. Add remaining water or *kuah Indonesia* and bring to a boil. Skim off any scum.

6. Simmer stock over very low heat for 5–6 hours.

Whenever you prepare crustaceans, save the shells in the freezer until you have enough to make a stock.

Kaldu Sayur (Vegetable Stock)

3 fresh ears of corn, shucked and husk reserved
3 tablespoons coconut oil
150 g *bumbu sayur* (page 9)
3 kaffir lime leaves, bruised
2 stalks lemongrass, bruised
100 g shallots, peeled and thinly sliced
200 g carrots, peeled and thinly sliced into matchsticks
100 g celery with leaves, thinly sliced
100 g leek, finely sliced
50 g shiitake mushrooms, finely sliced
100 g tomatoes, halved and sliced
100 g pumpkin, peeled and thinly sliced into matchsticks
2 litres water

1. Preheat oven to 175°C.
2. Cut corn into short lengths. Shred corn husk and scatter with corn pieces on a baking tray. Invert a cooling rack on corn and husk to hold them in place. Bake for about 20 minutes or until golden brown, turning corn over once or twice during baking.
3. Heat coconut oil in a saucepan and add *bumbu sayur*, kaffir lime leaves and lemongrass. Sauté for 2 minutes until fragrant.
4. Add baked corn and husk and remaining ingredients except water. Sauté for 5 minutes over medium heat.
5. Add water and bring to a boil. Skim off any scum.
6. Simmer stock over very low heat for 5–6 hours.

For a brown vegetable stock, toss ingredients together with corn in 3 tablespoons coconut oil, then roast in an oven at 220°C until golden brown. Cook as above.

Base Sate (Peanut Sauce)

500 g raw peanuts with skin, deep-fried or roasted golden brown
5 garlic cloves, peeled and sliced
8–10 bird's eye chillies, finely sliced
10 g ginger, peeled and very finely sliced
10 g galangal *(laos)*, peeled and finely sliced
1 litre coconut milk
20 g palm sugar, chopped
4 Tbsp sweet soy sauce *(kecap manis)*
2 kaffir lime leaves, torn
1 Tbsp lime juice
1 Tbsp fried shallots
salt, to taste

1. Combine peanuts, garlic, chillies, ginger and galangal in a stone mortar or food processor and grind finely.
2. Place ground ingredients in a heavy saucepan together with three-quarters coconut milk, palm sugar and sweet soy sauce. Bring to a boil, then reduce heat and simmer uncovered for 10 minutes, stirring frequently to prevent the sauce from sticking. Should the sauce become too thick, add the remaining coconut milk and, if necessary, a little more water.
3. Add lime juice and sprinkle with shallots just before serving as a dipping sauce for satay. Season to taste with salt.

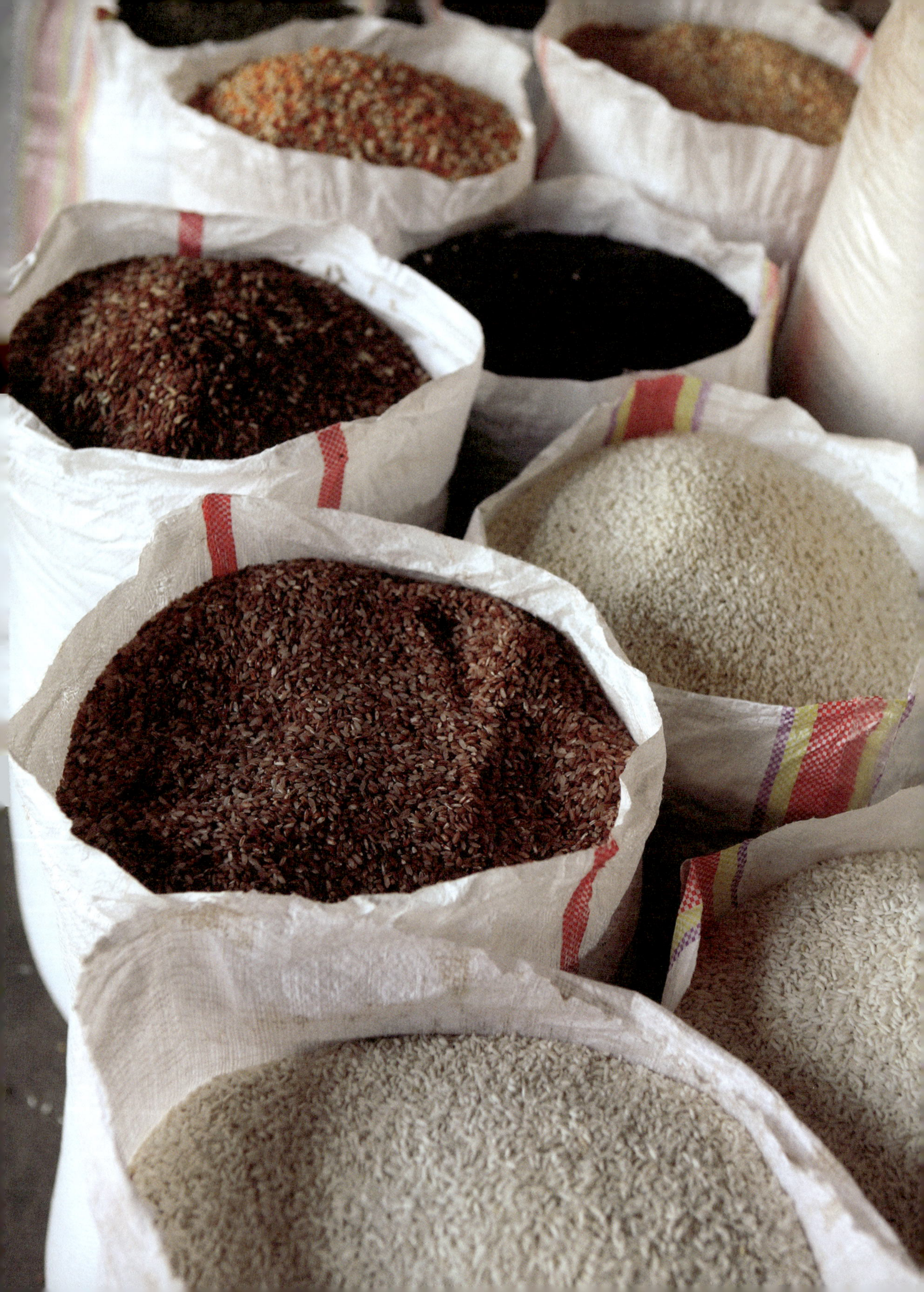

Rice & Soup

Nasi Kuning (Yellow Rice) 15

Nasi Goreng Mawut (Fried Rice with Noodles) 16

Papeda (Sun-dried Seafood Soup) 19

Ute Kentang (Oxtail Soup with Potatoes and Carrots) 20

Tek Wan (Prawn Noodle Soup) 23

Bakso Sampi (Beef Dumpling Noodle Soup) 24

Soto Ayam (Chicken Noodle Soup) 27

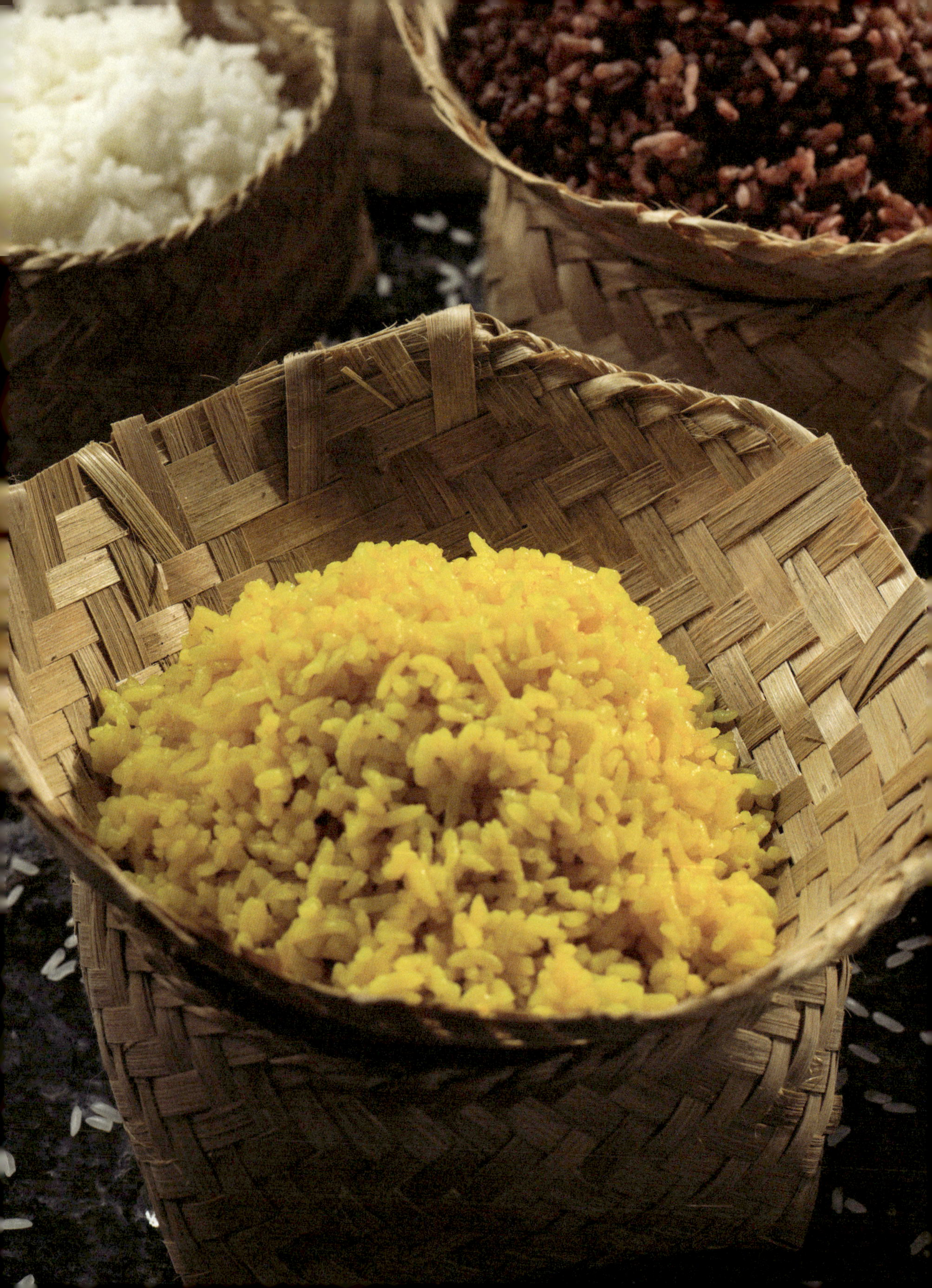

Nasi Kuning (Yellow Rice) Serves 4–5

Rice is extremely important in Indonesia's food culture and is often the centre of a meal served with other side dishes of vegetables, meat and soup.

250 g long-grain rice, rinsed and drained

DRESSING

2 tablespoons coconut oil
50 g shallots, peeled and chopped
25 g garlic, peeled and chopped
1 stalk lemongrass, bruised
2 *salam* leaves
1 stalk pandan leaf
375 ml *kuah Indonesia* (page 10)
75 ml turmeric water, made by blending 30 g freshly ground turmeric with 60 ml water and strained
125 ml coconut milk
salt and pepper, to taste

1. Soak cleaned rice for 25 minutes in fresh water.

2. Drain water and steam rice for 25 minutes.

3. Meanwhile, prepare dressing. Heat oil in a saucepan. Add shallots and garlic and sauté for 1 minute. Add lemongrass, *salam* and pandan leaves and sauté for another 1 minute.

4. Fill saucepan with *kuah Indonesia* and turmeric water and bring to a boil. Reduce heat and simmer for 1 minute. Add coconut milk and return to boil. Simmer for another 2 minutes, then season to taste with salt and pepper.

5. Pour steamed rice into a deep bowl and add boiling dressing.

6. Mix well and allow rice to absorb liquid.

7. Return rice to steamer and steam for another 25 minutes or until rice is done.

Nasi Goreng Mawut (Fried Rice with Noodles) Serves 4

This has to be my favourite version of the famous *nasi goreng*. Although it is not often cooked in private homes for local consumption, *nasi goreng* is a very popular street food treat for the Indonesians. The term literally means "fried rice" but it is different from the usual fried rice cooked in Chinese restaurants all over the world. There are almost as many varieties of it as there are small *warungs* (roadside food stalls) and cooks who prepare this dish.

- 100 g boneless chicken thighs, skin removed and cut into 1-cm cubes
- 2 tablespoons *bumbu daging* (page 8)
- 100 g prawns, peeled, cleaned, deveined and halved
- 2 tablespoons *bumbu ikan* (page 8)
- vegetable or coconut oil, as needed
- 50 g white cabbage, sliced
- 20 g large red chillies, halved, seeded and sliced
- 3–5 bird's eye chillies, finely sliced
- 1 tablespoon chilli sauce
- 2 tablespoons salty soy sauce *(kecap asin)*
- 50 g shiitake mushrooms, sliced
- 3 eggs, whisked thoroughly
- 300 g rice, cooked and cooled
- 300 g egg noodles, cooked and cooled
- 30 g spinach, cleaned and roughly sliced
- 30 g leek or spring onions (scallions), sliced
- 20 g celery leaves, sliced
- 2 tablespoons finely sliced lemon basil *(kemangi)*
- salt, to taste
- 2 tablespoons fried shallots

1. Marinate chicken with *bumbu daging* and prawns with *bumbu ikan*.
2. In separate frying pans, heat a little oil and quickly stir-fry chicken and prawns for 1 minute. Set aside and keep warm.
3. Heat 4 tablespoons oil in a wok or large non-stick frying pan. Add cabbage, red chillies and bird's eye chillies and fry over high heat for 1 minute.
4. Add chilli sauce and soy sauce and fry until almost dry.
5. Add shiitake mushrooms and fry for another minute.
6. Add eggs and continue to fry until eggs are scrambled and almost cooked.
7. Add rice, mix well and fry for 1 minute.
8. Add egg noodles, mix well and fry again for 2 more minutes over high heat.
9. Add spinach, leek or spring onions, celery leaves and lemon basil, mix well and fry for 1 more minute.
10. Remove from heat and season to taste with salt. Garnish as desired.

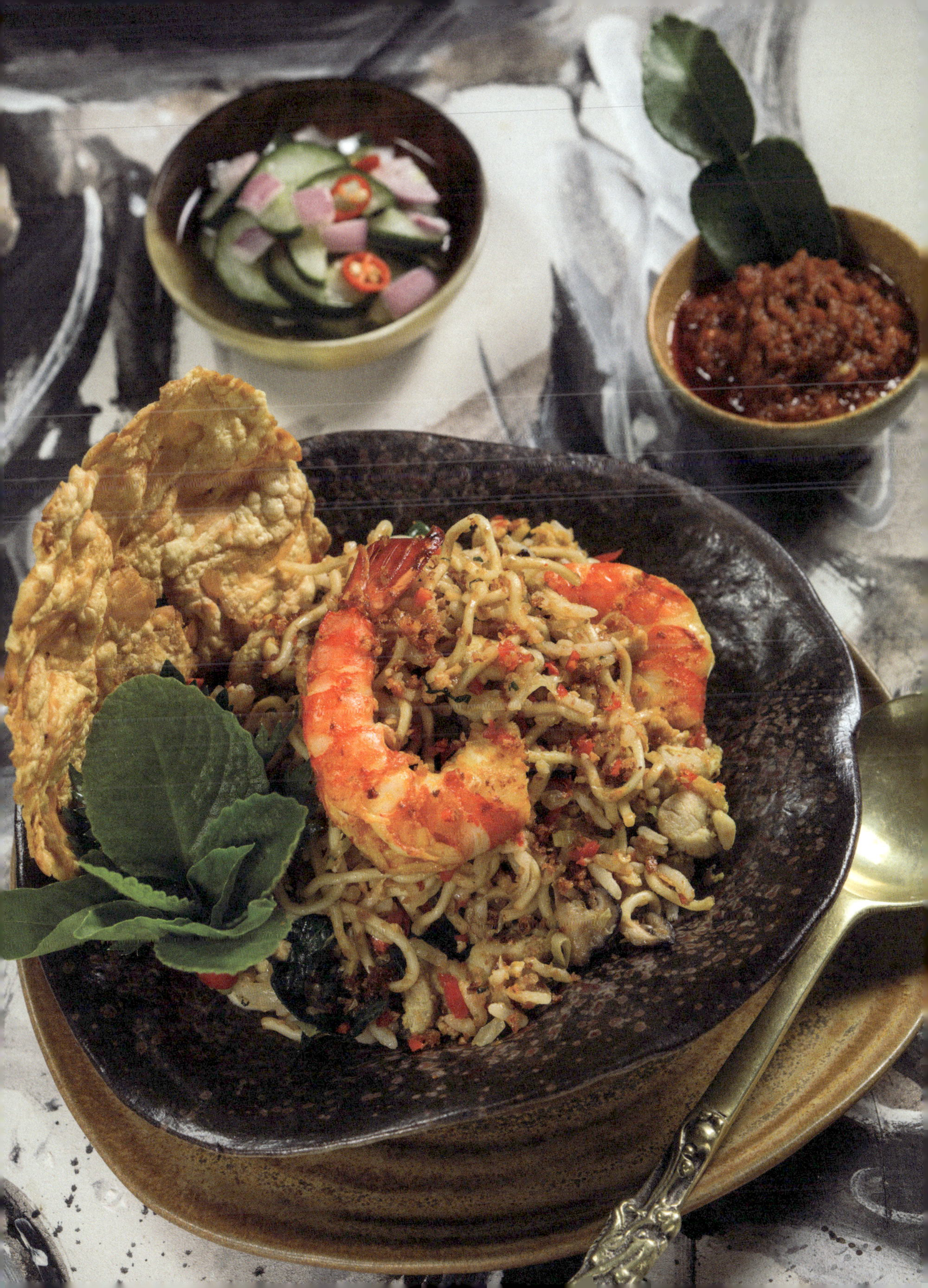

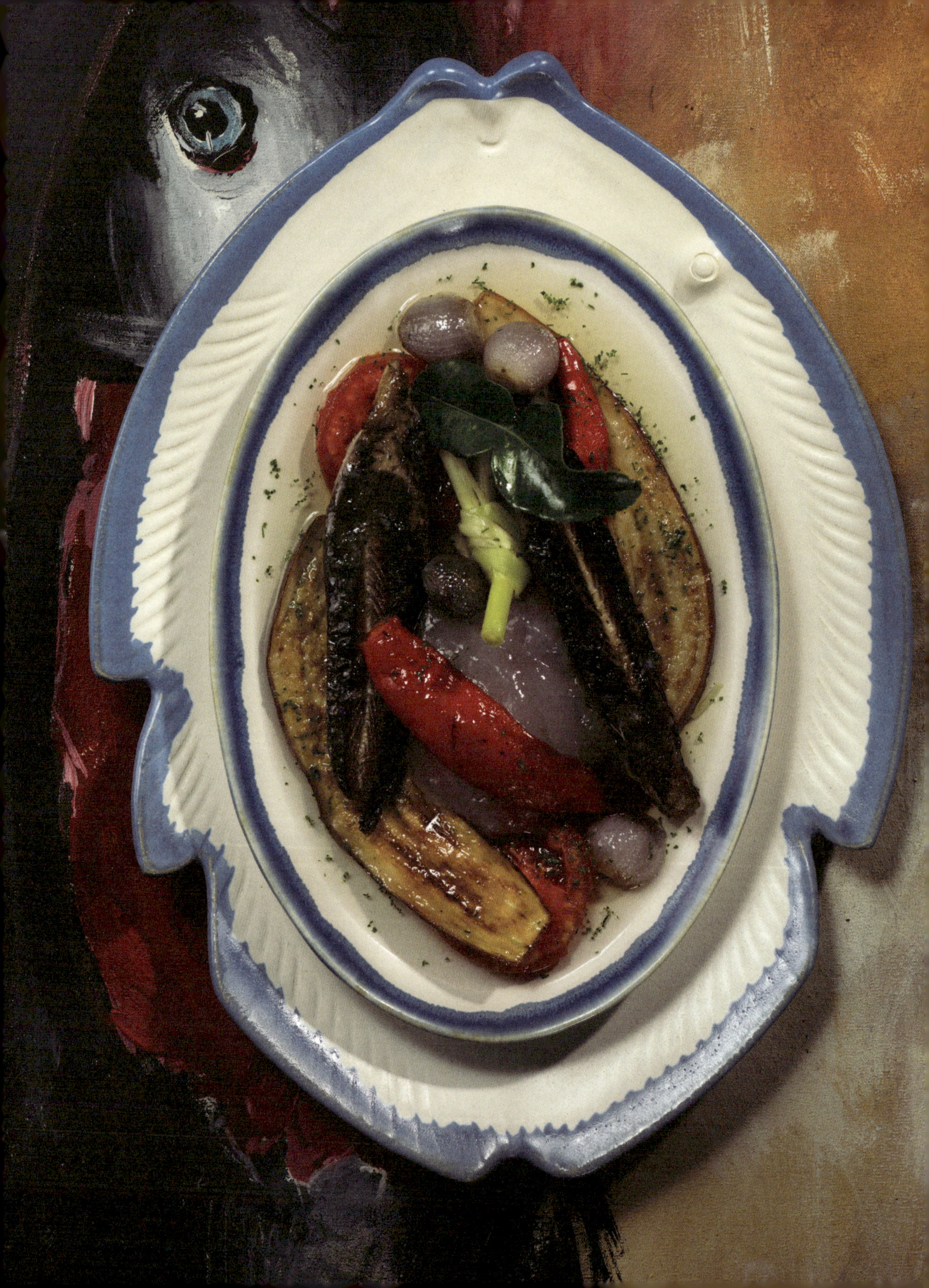

Papeda (Sun-dried Seafood Soup) Serves 6–8

This is the national dish of the Spice Islands. What makes it so special is the use of fresh sago, which in its natural form is almost impossible to find outside Asia. Sago has a jelly-like texture and is rather bland. The main reason for using sago in many dishes is the absence of rice. I personally prefer eating this delicious tasty seafood treat with a generous helping of steamed rice or freshly steamed rice cakes.

1 tablespoon salt + more to taste
4 tablespoons coconut oil
4 medium eggplants, halved
600 g whole dried mackerels or dry shaved bonito
20 medium shallots, grilled, skins removed, halved and grilled
4 medium tomatoes, peeled, seeded, grilled and halved
4 large red chillies, grilled, skinned and seeded
2 stalks lemongrass, bruised
3 kaffir lime leaves, bruised
2 tablespoons lime juice + more to taste
1 tablespoon sugar
1.5 litres) water or *kuah Indonesia* or *kaldu udang* (page 10)
100 g sago flour
crushed white peppercorns, to taste

1. Combine 1 tablespoon salt and 4 tablespoons coconut oil and blend well. Brush eggplants evenly with salt-oil mix and marinate for 10 minutes or pan-fry in a hot non-stick pan. Grill eggplants over medium hot charcoal until soft and evenly browned. Place into a large soup kettle.

2. Grill mackerels or bonito over a medium hot grill until golden. Add to soup kettle.

3. Add shallots, tomatoes, chillies, lemongrass, kaffir lime leaves, lime juice and sugar.

4. Bring 1 litre water or *kuah Indonesia* or *kaldu udang* to boil and pour into soup kettle. Allow ingredients to infuse for 1 hour.

5. In the meantime, bring remaining 500 ml water or *kuah Indonesia* or *kaldu udang* to boil. Place sago flour into a mixing bowl and pour boiling liquid over while rapidly mixing with a spatula or whisk. As liquid slowly cools, it will gradually thicken into a soft elastic paste. To serve, take two chopsticks (chopsticks works best) and immerse one into sago paste. Start rolling with the help of the other chopstick into an oblong lump. Place into individual serving dishes.

6. Strain liquid into a pot and return to a boil. Season to taste with salt, crushed white peppercorns and more lime juice.

7. Evenly divide eggplants, tomatoes, chillies, shallots and grilled fish among serving dishes and pour broth over. Serve.

Ute Kentang (Oxtail Soup with Potatoes and Carrots)
Serves 6

This dish originated from Flores and is often prepared for celebrations. Water buffaloes can be used in place of beef for the preparation of this dish.

60 ml water

2 stalks lemongrass, bruised

¾ tablespoon salt

4 *salam* leaves

90 ml coconut or vegetable oil

1.2 kg oxtail, cut into 2-cm pieces and thoroughly cleaned

1.5 litres *kuah Indonesia* (page 10)

400 g potatoes, peeled and cut into 2 x 1-cm cubes

300 g carrots

salt, to taste

crushed white peppercorns, to taste

40 g spring onions (scallions), sliced into 3-cm lengths

fried shallots, to garnish

SPICE BLEND

100 g large red chillies halved, seeded and sliced

3–5 bird's eye chillies, finely sliced

30 g garlic, peeled and sliced

60 g shallots, peeled and sliced

30 g ginger, peeled and sliced

30 g galangal *(laos)*, peeled and sliced

30 g turmeric, peeled and sliced

20 g candlenuts

1 teaspoon crushed black peppercorns

½ teaspoon crushed coriander seeds

½ teaspoon caraway seeds

¼ teaspoon ground nutmeg

20 g palm sugar, chopped

45 ml coconut oil

1. Prepare spice blend. Combine all ingredients in a stone mortar or food processor and grind into a fine paste.

2. Place ground ingredients into a pressure cooker pot and add water, lemongrass, salt and 2 *salam* leaves. Simmer over medium heat for approximately 2 minutes.

3. Heat oil in saucepan until very hot. Sear oxtail evenly until golden. Drain half of oil. Add oxtail into a pressure cooker pot and mix well with spice paste. Add hot *kuah Indonesia* and remaining *salam* leaves and bring to a boil. Remove scum.

4. Pressure cook at 1 bar / 15 psi for 90 minutes. Turn off heat and allow pot to cool for 30 minutes.

5. Strain 1 litre of *kuah Indonesia* into a small casserole and cook potatoes and carrots separately in it, simmering slowly until just cooked.

6. Drain oxtail from *kuah Indonesia* and remove meat from bones. Cut into even cubes. Bring remaining *kuah Indonesia* to a simmer and season with salt and crushed white peppercorns.

7. Add potatoes, carrots, oxtail and spring onions. Simmer again for 2 minutes.

8. Dish out and garnish with fried shallots.

9. Serve with rice, rice cakes, *saus pedas tomat* (page 9), lime wedges and cassava crackers.

If a pressure cooker is not available, use a traditional soup pan or stockpot. Simmer oxtail over very low heat for approximately 5–6 hours, or until the meat is very tender and comes easily off the bones.

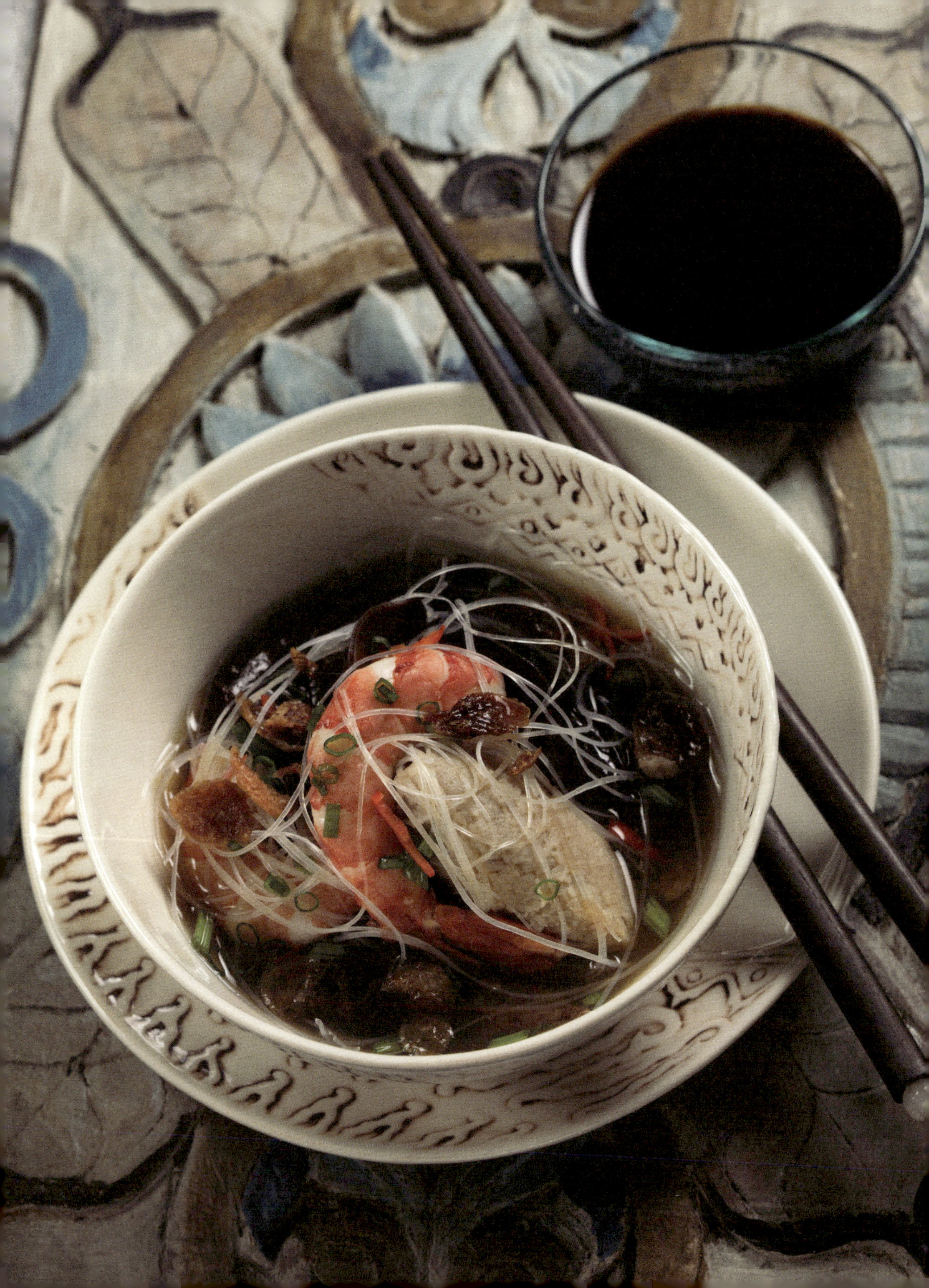

Tek Wan (Prawn Noodle Soup) Serves 6–8

This dish originates from South Sumatra and has very strong Chinese elements.

1.5 litres *kaldu udang* or *kuah Indonesia* (page 10)

200 g medium prawns, peeled, deveined and halved

120 g glass noodles

50 g dried wood ear mushrooms, soaked in warm water for 15 minutes

5 tablespoons finely sliced spring onions (scallions)

4 tablespoons coarsely chopped fried shallots

SEAFOOD DUMPLINGS

150 g mackerel fillets, minced

1 tablespoon tapioca flour

50 ml coconut cream

50 ml *kaldu udang* or *kuah Indonesia* (page 10)

1 tablespoon freshly chopped coriander

1 tablespoon oyster sauce

1 teaspoon sweet soy sauce (*kecap manis*)

1 teaspoon salty soy sauce (*kecap asin*)

1 pinch ground white pepper

1 pinch sugar

1 pinch salt

DRESSING

5 tablespoons rice vinegar

5 tablespoons sweet soy sauce (*kecap manis*)

5 tablespoons salty soy sauce (*kecap asin*)

salt, to taste

1. Prepare seafood dumplings. Combine all ingredients and mix well into a smooth paste.

2. Make dumplings using two tablespoons to shape fish paste into even oblongs.

3. Bring *kaldu udang* or *kuah Indonesia* to a simmer and cook dumplings for 5 minutes or until they float to the surface. Place dumplings in serving bowls and set aside.

4. Place prawns into a soup strainer and cook for 1 minute in simmering *kaldu udang* or *kuah Indonesia*. Place into serving bowls with dumplings.

5. Heat noodles briefly in *kaldu udang* or *kuah Indonesia*. Divide among prepared serving bowls.

6. Cut wood ear mushrooms into even pieces and poach in *kaldu udang* or *kuah Indonesia* for 1 minute. Ladle soup with wood ear mushrooms into serving bowls.

7. Garnish with sliced spring onions and fried shallots.

8. Combine all ingredients for dressing and serve on the side with noodle soup.

Bakso Sampi (Beef Dumpling Noodle Soup) Serves 6

Indonesians love snacks. Little food stalls called *warung* are found in every village neighbourhood. Some serve full meals and many serve a range of soups, and stay open late into the night.

STOCK

3 kg chicken bones, without fat and skin cut into small pieces or beef bones or beef trimmings, cut into small pieces

250 g *bumbu daging* (page 8)

3 large red chillies

5–7 birds eye chillies, bruised

4 stalks lemongrass, bruised

5 kaffir lime leaves, bruised

5 *salam* leaves

2 tablespoons crushed roasted coriander seeds

2 tablespoons crushed black peppercorns

8 cloves

salt, to taste

BEEF DUMPLINGS

150 g beef, top side minced

10 g spring onions (scallions), sliced

1 tablespoon oyster sauce

1 teaspoon sweet soy sauce (*kecap manis*)

1 teaspoon salty soy sauce (*kecap asin*)

1 tablespoon potato flour

1 pinch ground white pepper

1 pinch salt

1 pinch ground nutmeg

16 wanton wrappers

120 g egg noodles, cooked

120 g fried bean curd, sliced

Chinese celery leaves, to garnish

fried shallots, to garnish

1. Prepare stock. Rinse bones until water is clear. Place bones in a stockpot, cover with cold water and bring to a boil over high heat. Drain and discard water. Rinse bones again under running water.

2. Return bones to a pressure cooker, add three times as much water (*kuah Indonesia* would be preferred) as bones and return to a boil. Once liquid comes to a simmer, remove scum. Add all ingredients and cover pressure cooker with lid. Pressure cook at a gauge of 1 bar / 15 psi for 2 hours. Start timing as soon as full pressure has been reached. Turn off heat. Allow the cooker to depressurize by cooling for 45 minutes.

3. Strain liquid and discard solids.

4. Prepare beef dumplings. Combine minced beef and all ingredients except wanton wrappers and mix well into a smooth paste. Season to taste.

5. Place one teaspoon of paste in centre of a wanton wrapper and fold sides up. Repeat with the rest of the ingredients.

6. Place 8 dumplings into simmering stock and poach for 3 minutes (Alternatively, steam for 3 minutes.)

7. Deep-fry another 8 beef dumplings in medium hot oil until crispy. Drain on kitchen towels.

8. Shape remaining paste with the help of two tablespoons into even dumplings. Place into simmering stock and poach for 2 minutes.

9. To serve one portion of soup, bring 1.5 litres of stock to a boil. Divide dumplings, noodles and bean curd among four large soup bowls and fill with boiling stock.

10. Garnish with sliced Chinese celery leaves and fried shallots. Serve.

If you prefer a more conventional way of preparing the stock, use a traditional stockpot and simmer stock over very low heat for 6–7 hours, frequently removing scum as it accumulates.

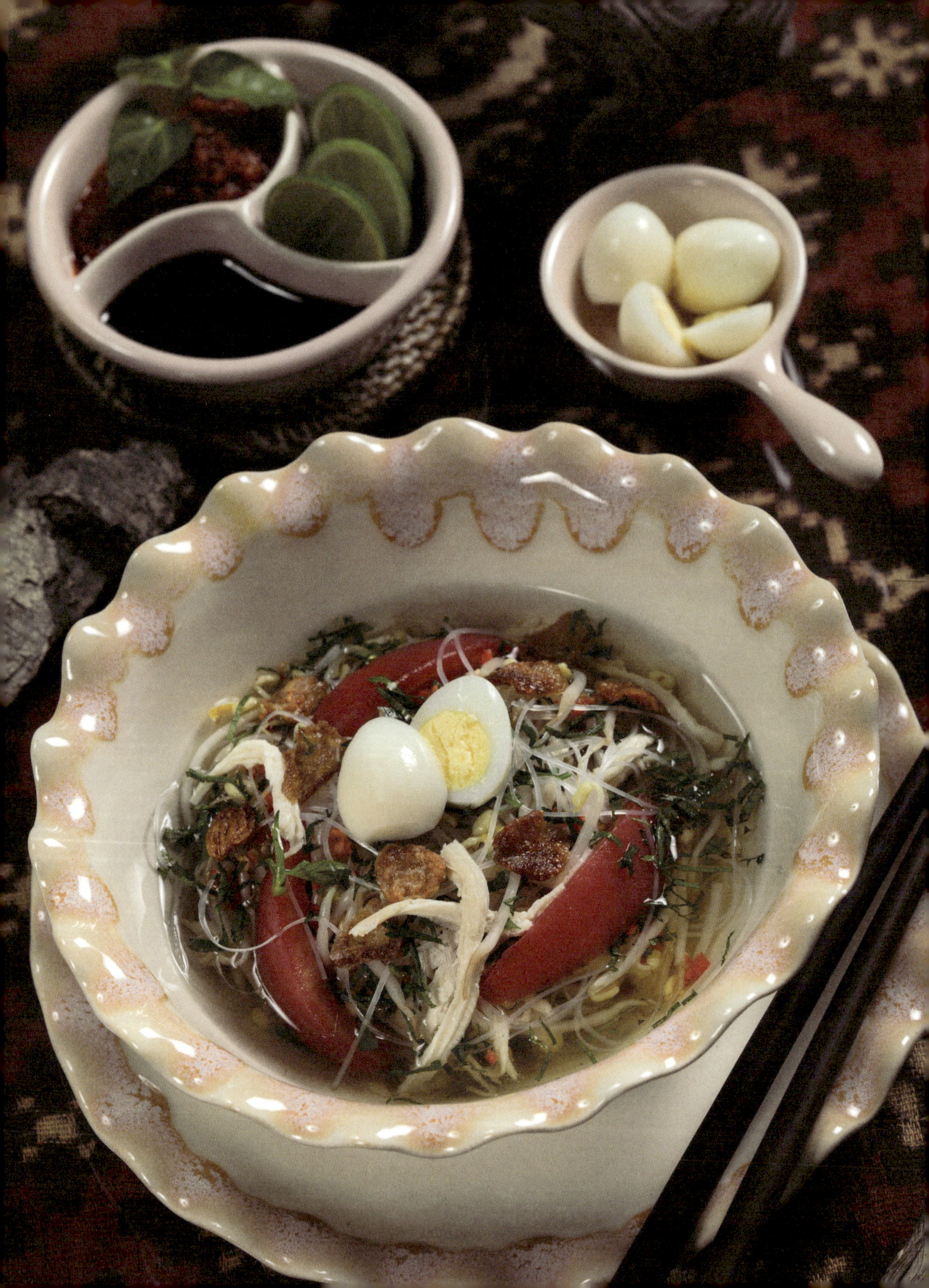

Soto Ayam (Chicken Noodle Soup) Serves 4

This has to be Indonesia's most prepared soup and it can be commonly found at many food stalls.

2 stalks lemongrass, bruised

3 kaffir lime leaves, bruised

3 *salam* leaves or kaffir lime leaves

2 litres *kuah Indonesia* (page 10)

1.2 kg chicken, cleaned and pat dry

salt, to taste

100 g glass noodles, soaked in warm water to soften

50 g bean sprouts, blanched for 15 seconds and drained

50 g Chinese celery leaves, finely sliced

4 hard-boiled quail eggs, peeled and halved

2 tomatoes, cut into wedges

2 tablespoons fried shallots

SPICE BLEND

2 tablespoons coconut or vegetable oil

80 g shallots, peeled and sliced

50 g garlic, peeled and sliced

30 g ginger, peeled and sliced

30 g galangal *(laos)*, peeled and sliced

30 g turmeric, peeled and sliced

20 g candlenuts, roasted and crushed

3–5 bird's eye chillies, sliced

½ teaspoon crushed black peppercorns

1. Prepare spice blend. Combine all ingredients in a stone mortar or food processor and grind into a very fine paste.

2. Transfer ground spices to a pressure cooker pot and add lemongrass, *salam* or kaffir lime leaves. Sauté over medium heat until fragrant.

3. Fill pot with *kuah Indonesia* and bring to a simmer. Remove scum.

4. Add chicken and bring to simmer. Cover pot and pressure-cook at 1 bar / 15 psi for 45 minutes. Start timing once full pressure is reached. Turn off heat and allow pot to cool for 30 minutes.

5. Remove chicken from *kuah Indonesia* and carefully debone. Shred meat into fine strips by hand.

6. Strain *kuah Indonesia* and bring to a simmer. Season to taste with salt.

7. Briefly blanch glass noodles and cool in iced water. Drain. Heat noodles for a few seconds in simmering *kuah Indonesia* before serving.

8. To serve, place shredded chicken, bean sprouts and celery leaves in a soup strainer and heat for 1 minute in simmering *kuah Indonesia*. Arrange on top of glass noodles. Add chicken soup and garnish with hard-boiled quail egg, tomato wedges and fried shallots. Serve with *saus pedas tomat* (page 9) and lime wedges.

Instead of a pressure cooker, follow the steps above using a traditional stockpot and simmer stock for 6–7 hours.

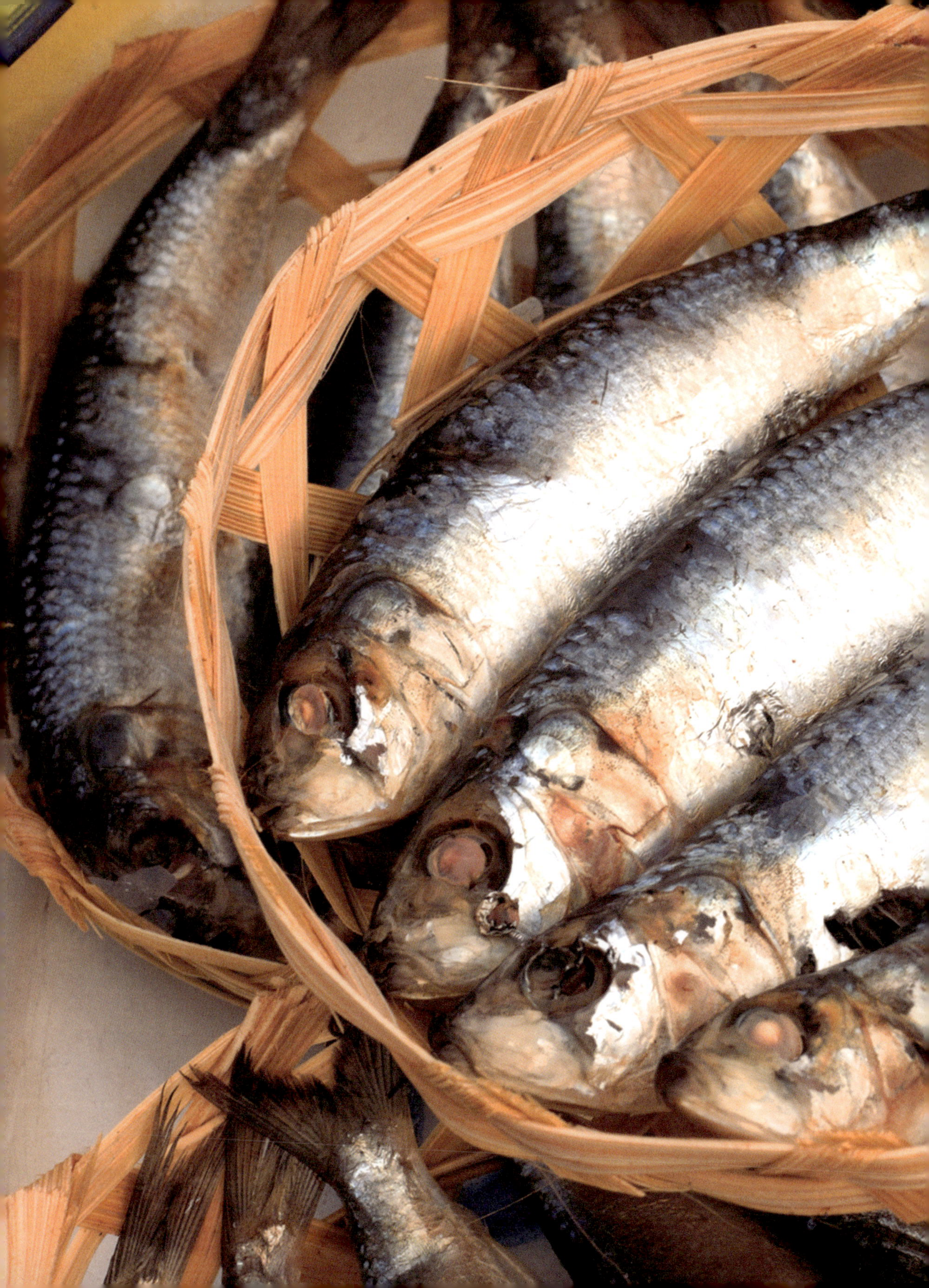

Seafood

Otak Otak (Minced Fish Steamed in Banana Leaf) 30

Pepes Udang Karang Jamur
(Lobster and Mushrooms in Banana Leaf) 33

Udang Balado (Prawns in Tomato Sauce) 34

Sambal Udang (Prawns in Spiced Tomato Sauce) 37

Ikan Bakar Saus Tomat
(Grilled Seafood with Shallot Lemongrass Dressing) 38

Rendang Kerang (Mussels Braised in Spiced Coconut Milk) 41

Kepiting Kuning (Crab in Yellow Turmeric Dressing) 42

Otak Otak (Minced Fish Steamed in Banana Leaf) Serves 6–8

South Sulawesi is known for Coto's various types of beef soups and *otak otak*, and Makassar Ibu Elli is renowned nationwide for serving the best *otak otak*. Up to 10,000 of these delicate fish parcels are prepared daily by a team of ladies that still follow traditional techniques and preparation methods. Most visitors will not only stop by to enjoy a quick snack but will also bring a takeaway box home for their loved ones.

200 ml coconut cream
50 g sago flour
800 g mackerel fillet, skinned and minced
100 ml light *kaldu udang* or *kuah Indonesia* (page 10)
2 tablespoons lime juice
50 g spring onions (scallions), finely sliced
salt, to taste
16 banana leaves, cut into 20-cm squares

SPICE PASTE
80 g shallots, peeled and sliced
20 g garlic, peeled and sliced
3–5 bird's eye chillies, finely sliced
ground white pepper, to taste
salt, to taste

1. Prepare spice paste. Combine all ingredients in a stone mortar or food processor and grind into a very fine paste.

2. Combine coconut cream and sago flour and whisk into a smooth mixture.

3. Combine minced fish, *kaldu udang* or *kuah Indonesia*, spice paste and coconut cream mixture in a food processor and blend into a very smooth paste. Add lime juice and spring onions. Season to taste with salt.

4. Place 2 tablespoonfuls fish paste in centre of each banana leaf square. Fold two opposite sides of banana leaf over to enclose filling tightly. Secure open ends with bamboo skewers. Repeat until ingredients are used up.

5. Steam parcels for 4 minutes, then place on a charcoal grill and cook for 3 more minutes until banana leaves are evenly browned.

6. Serve with *saus pedas tomat* (page 9) and lime wedges.

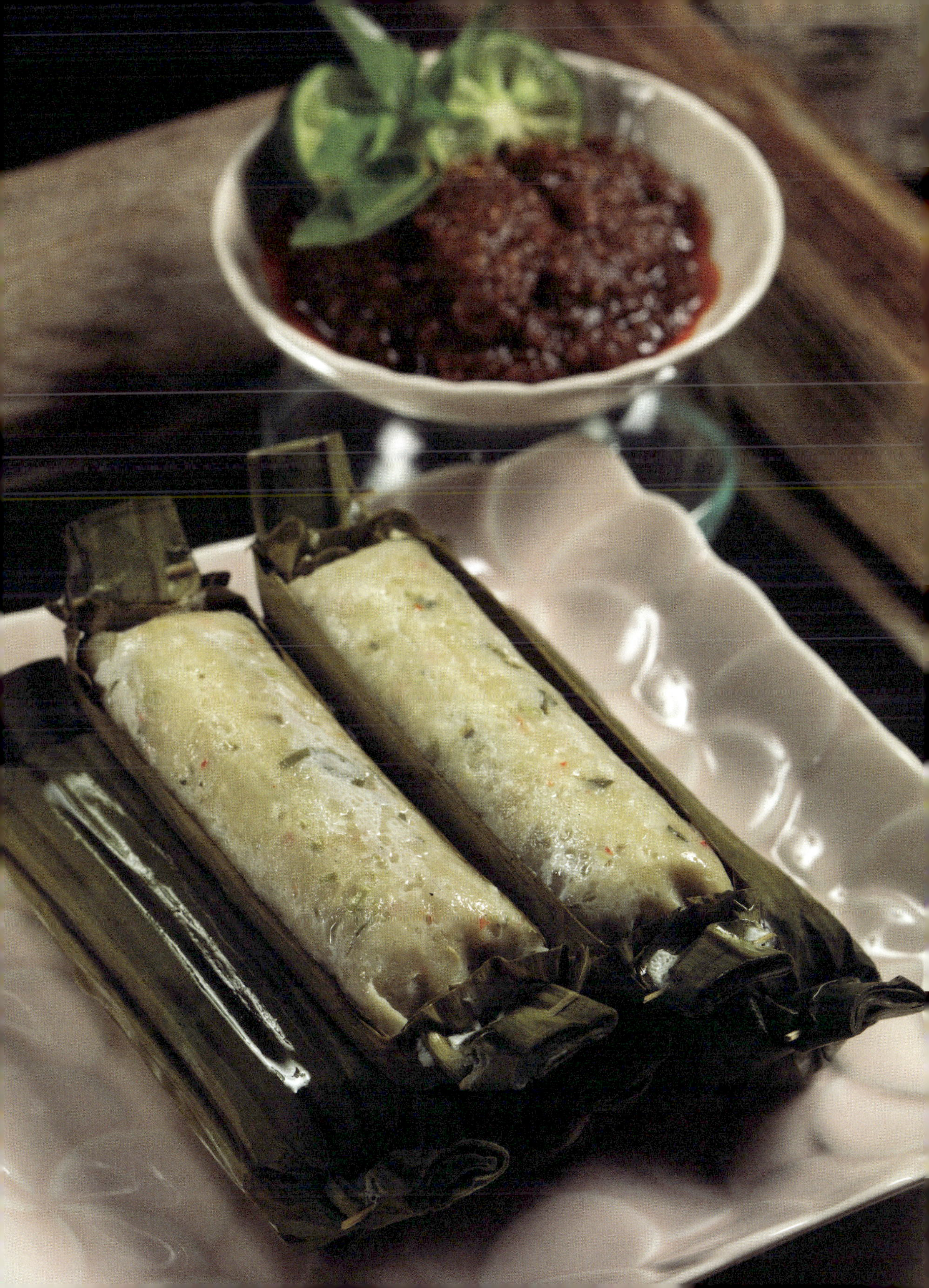

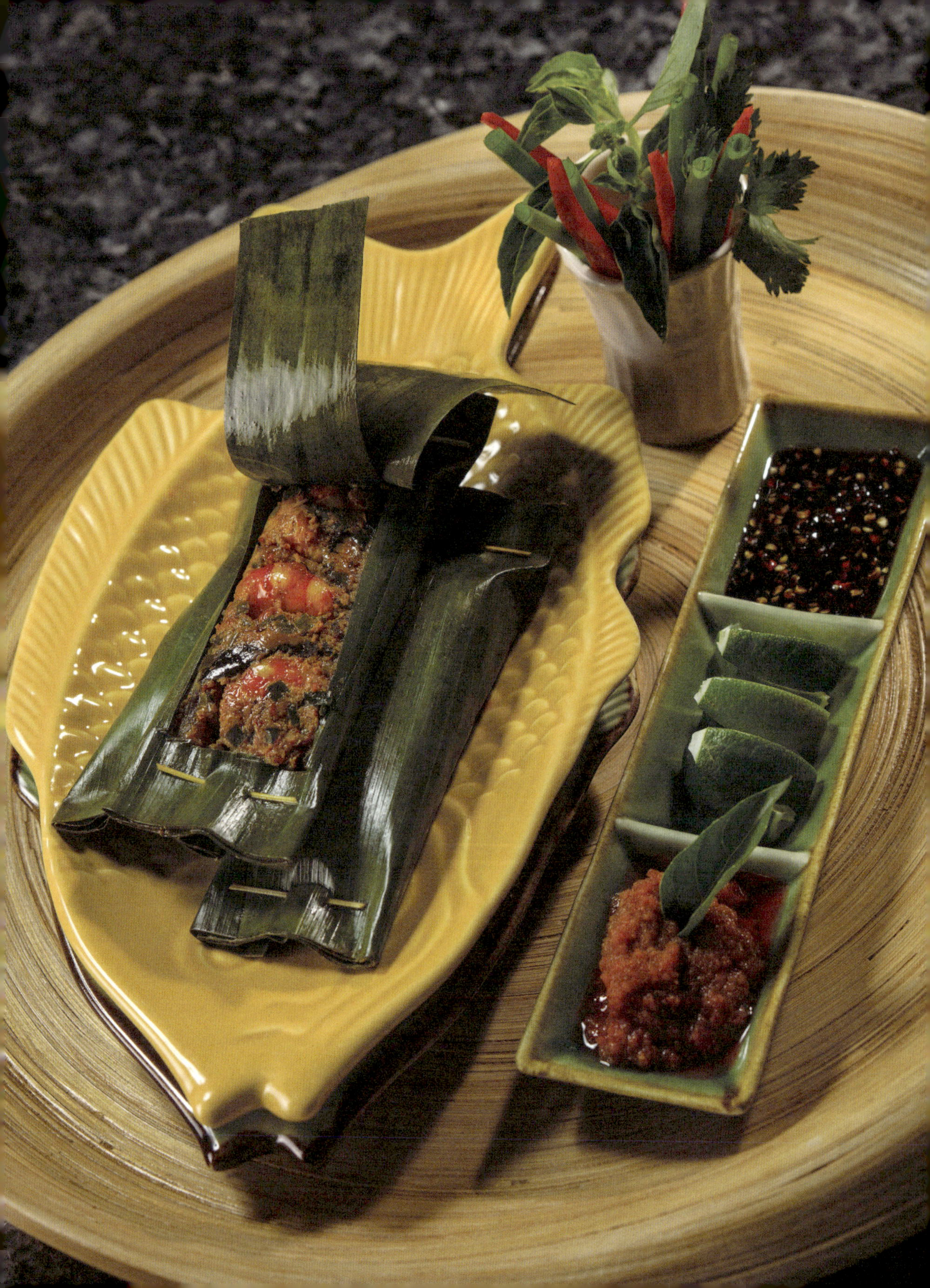

Pepes Udang Karang Jamur (Lobster and Mushrooms in Banana Leaf) Serves 4–6

This dish originates from the eastern islands of Indonesia. Lobsters can be replaced with prawns or any firm white fish and shiitake mushrooms can be replaced with any of your favourite mushrooms.

3 tablespoons coconut or vegetable oil

600 g raw lobster meat or prawns or crabs, cut into 1.5-cm cubes

125 g shiitake mushrooms, sliced

2 eggs, beaten

60 ml coconut cream

50 g spring onions (scallions), finely sliced

salt, to taste

crushed white peppercorns, to taste

8 banana leaves, cut into 25 x 18-cm sheets

8 kaffir lime leaves, bruised

SPICE PASTE

30 g garlic, peeled and sliced

50 g shallots, peeled and sliced

30 g ginger, peeled and sliced

30 g turmeric, peeled and sliced

60 g large red chillies, halved, seeded and sliced

3–5 bird's eye chillies, finely sliced

salt, to taste

1. Prepare spice paste. Combine all ingredients in a stone mortar or food processor and grind into a fine paste.

2. Heat oil in heavy saucepan. Add spice paste and sauté over medium heat until fragrant. Allow spice paste to cool to room temperature.

3. Combine spice paste with all remaining ingredients except banana and kaffir lime leaves in a deep mixing bowl and mix well until lobster and mushrooms are well coated.

4. Place each banana leaf sheet over an open gas flame or boiling water for a few seconds to soften the banana leaves and so that the leaves do not tear when folded.

5. Place a kaffir lime leaf in the centre of a banana leaf and top with two tablespoons of lobster-mushroom mix. Fold long edges of banana leaf in towards the centre to enclose filling. Secure open ends with bamboo skewers or toothpicks.

6. Steam parcels for 4 minutes, then grill for 3 minutes over very low heat until a meat thermometer inserted into the parcels reads 50°C.

Udang Balado (Prawns in Tomato Sauce) Serves 4

This dish originates from West Sumatra, where the richly spiced dishes are either fiery hot or smothered in coconut milk. Known collectively as Padang food, these dishes are not only delicious, but also keep well and can withstand reheating.

1 kg large prawns, peeled and deveined
3 tablespoons lime juice
salt, to taste
ground white pepper, to taste
40 g rice flour
cooking oil, as needed

SAUCE
3 tablespoons coconut oil
50 g shallots, peeled and sliced
30 g garlic, peeled and sliced
2 kaffir lime leaves
50 g large red chillies, halved, seeded and sliced
5–7 bird's eye chillies, finely sliced
100 g tomatoes, quickly grilled, peeled, halved, seeded and diced
2 tablespoons tamarind juice

1. Mix prawns well with lime juice, salt and pepper. Let sit for 30 minutes.

2. Dust prawns evenly with rice flour.

3. Heat oil in a pan and pan-fry over medium heat until golden. Dish out and set aside.

4. Prepare sauce. Heat oil in heavy saucepan and sauté shallots, garlic, kaffir lime leaves, red chillies and bird's eye chillies over medium heat for 2 minutes.

5. Add tomatoes and tamarind juice and continue to sauté for 2 more minutes.

6. Season to taste with salt and pepper.

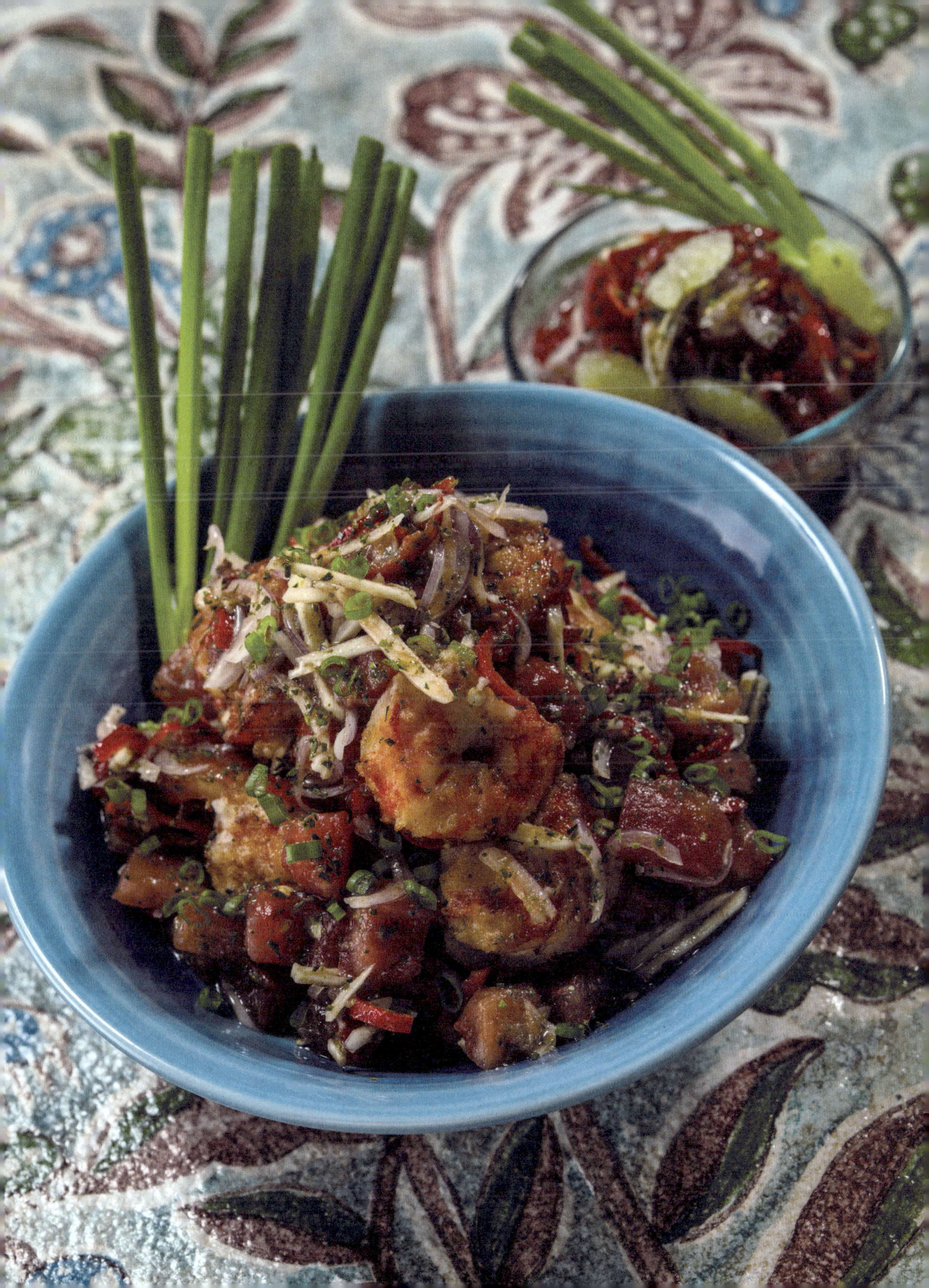

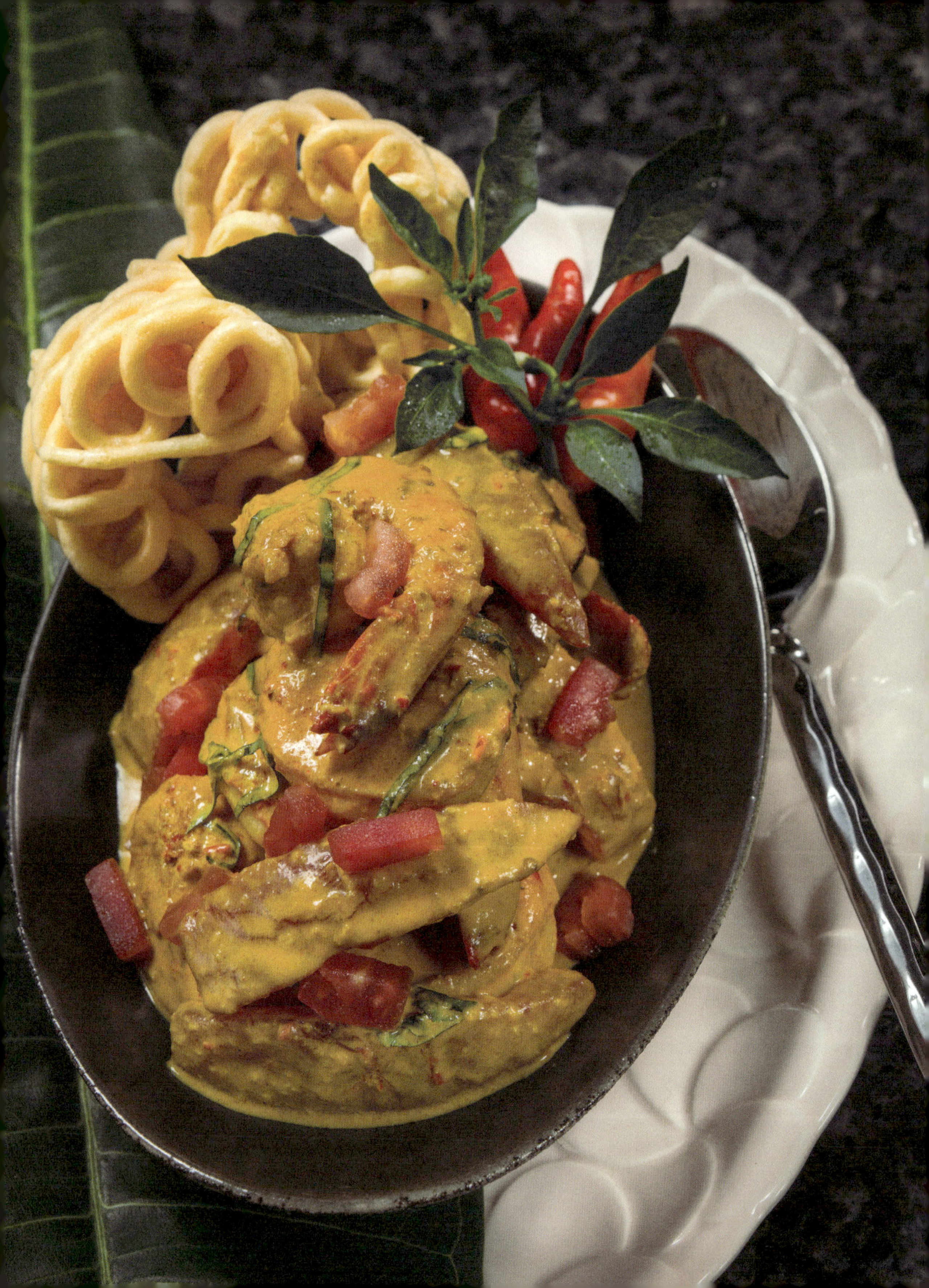

Sambal Udang (Prawns in Spiced Tomato Sauce) Serves 4–6

Any seafood tastes delicious when prepared this way– squid, mussels, crab or fish fillets would all well with this recipe. As with any other meat or seafood dish, take the protein out of refrigeration at least one hour before cooking and allow it to warm to room temperature.

150 g *bumbu ikan* (page 8)

800 g large prawns, peeled and deveined

30 ml vegetable or coconut oil

15 g *saus pedas tomat* (page 9)

1 stalk lemongrass, bruised

3 kaffir lime leaves, bruised

1 small sour star fruit (carambola), crushed or sliced

3 bird's eye chillies, whole (optional)

200 ml *kuah Indonesia* or *kaldu udang* (page 10)

100 ml coconut cream

150 g tomatoes, peeled, seeded and cut into small wedges

zest and juice of 1 lime, to taste

salt, to taste

1. Add half the *bumbu ikan* to the prawns and mix well.

2. Heat oil in a saucepan. Add prawns and sear prawns quickly on both sides until colour changes.

3. Add remaining *bumbu ikan*, *saus pedas tomat*, lemongrass, kaffir lime leaves, sour star fruit and bird's eye chillies, if used, and mix well. Continue to sauté for 1 more minute.

4. Add *kuah Indonesia* or *kaldu udang*, mix well and bring to simmer for 1 minute, frequently turning prawns over.

5. Add coconut cream, mix well and simmer for 1 more minute, frequently turning prawns.

6. Add tomato wedges, mix well and simmer for 1 minute.

7. Season to taste with lime zest and juice and salt. Garnish as desired.

Ikan Bakar Saus Tomat (Grilled Seafood with Shallot Lemongrass Dressing) Serves 6

Grilling over an open fire or glowing charcoal is the world's oldest cooking method, and this is really the key to achieve this delicate flavour in this dish.

- 1.2 kg assorted seafood (prawns, clams, mussels etc.) or 4 whole fish (snapper, trevally, mackerel etc.)
- 2 tablespoons lime juice + more for seasoning
- 1 teaspoon salt + more for seasoning
- 1 teaspoon finely crushed black pepper + more for seasoning
- 360 g *bumbu ikan* (page 8)

SHALLOT LEMONGRASS DRESSING
- 50 g shallots, peeled, halved and finely sliced
- 1 pinch salt + more to taste
- 50 g lemongrass, bruised, finely sliced and chopped
- 4–7 bird's eye chillies finely sliced (add more for a fiery taste)
- 1 teaspoon kaffir lime leaves, finely chopped
- ¼ teaspoon finely crumbled roasted shrimp paste *(terasi)*
- 3 tablespoons coconut oil
- lime juice, to taste

1. Prepare shallot and lemongrass dressing. Combine shallots and salt in deep bowl and mix thoroughly for 3 minutes. Add all remaining ingredients and blend well. Heat oil in a heavy saucepan. Add shallot lemongrass blend and sauté over high heat for 1 minute.

2. If using assorted seafood, marinate with salt, pepper, lime juice and three-quarters of *bumbu ikan*. Set aside one-quarter of *bumbu ikan* for basting mix.

3. If using whole fish, cut fish into halves butterfly-style starting at head and working towards tail. Make 4 slits, each about 1-cm deep, on side with bones. Seasons both sides of fish with lime juice, salt and pepper. Spread *bumbu ikan* evenly all over.

4. Brush assorted seafood or whole fish with a little basting mix before grilling over very hot glowing charcoal. Turn and baste frequently.

5. Serve with *saus pedas tomat* (page 9), shallot lemongrass dressing, lime wedges and lots of steamed rice.

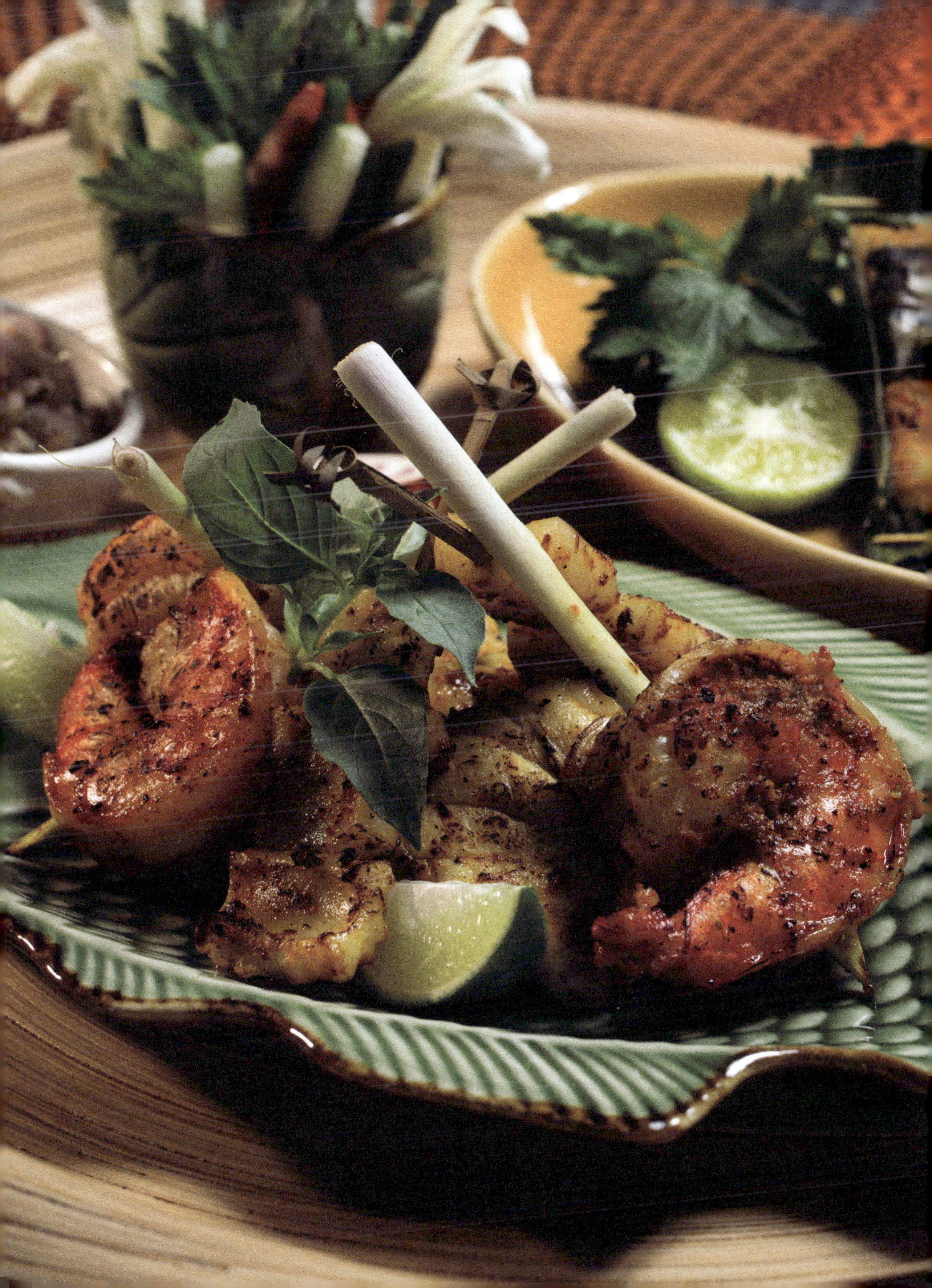

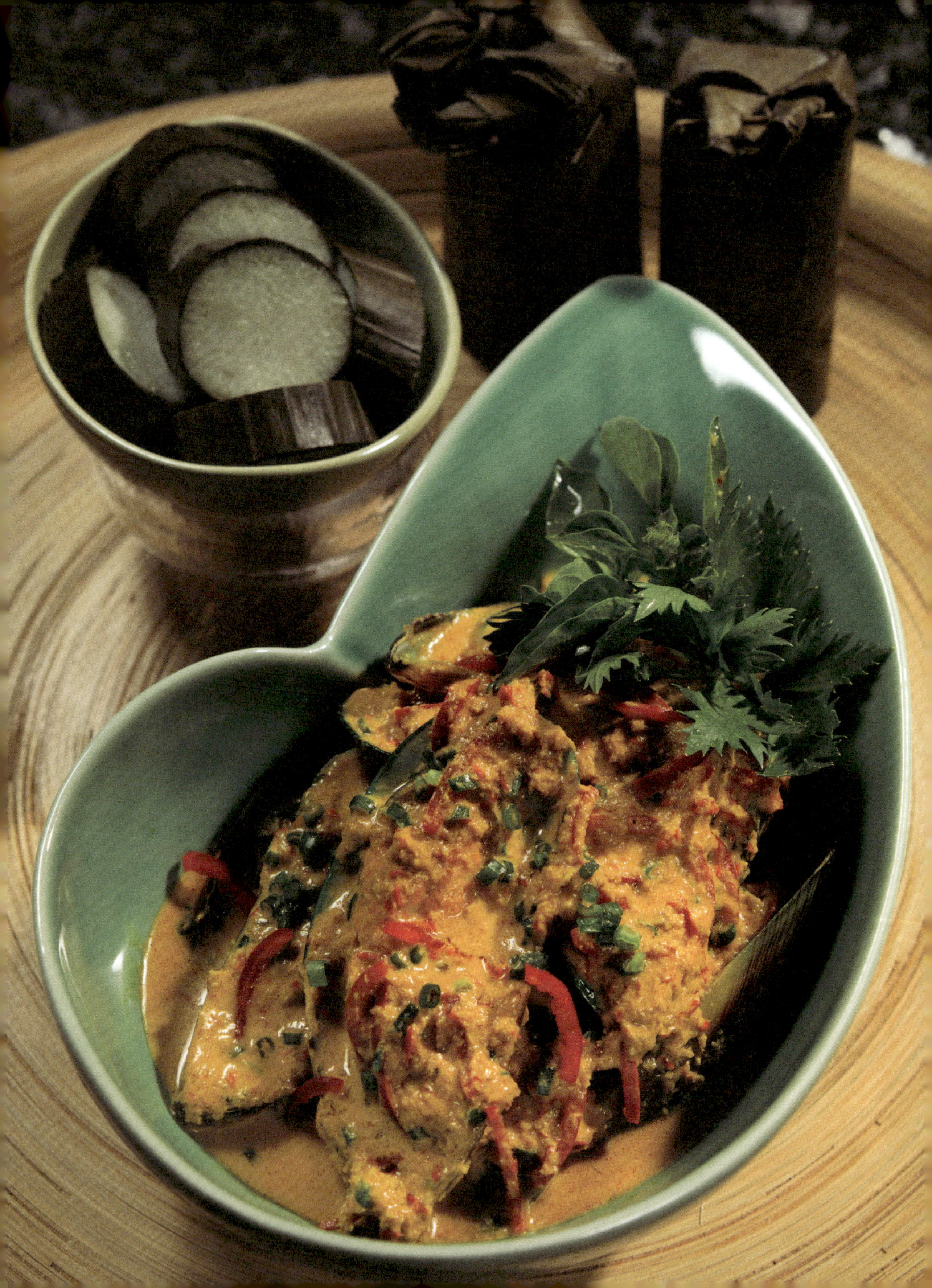

Rendang Kerang (Mussels Braised in Spiced Coconut Milk) Serves 4–6

When buying fresh mussels, the tightly closed live ones are what you are looking for. They are best kept in ice covered with a damp cloth, and should not sit in a puddle of melted water. Before cooking, scrub the shells with a solid brush and tear off the beard protruding out of the shell. Rinse well.

2 kg mussels, cleaned
250 ml *kuah Indonesia* (page 10)
125 ml coconut cream
2 *salam* leaves
2 kaffir lime leaves, bruised
1 turmeric leaf, bruised
1 pinch ground nutmeg
2 stalks lemongrass, bruised
2 tablespoons lime juice + more to taste
½ teaspoon sugar
salt, to taste
ground white pepper, to taste

SPICE PASTE
3 tablespoons coconut oil
80 g shallots, peeled and sliced
50 g garlic, peeled and sliced
50 g ginger, peeled and sliced
50 g turmeric, peeled and sliced
100 g large red chillies, halved, seeded and sliced
4 bird's eye chillies, sliced

1. Prepare spice paste. Combine all ingredients in a stone mortar or food processor and grind into a fine paste. Transfer to a heavy saucepan and sauté over medium heat until fragrant.

2. Increase heat, add mussels and stir well until mussels are evenly coated with spice paste.

3. Fill saucepan with *kuah Indonesia* and coconut cream, then add *salam*, kaffir lime and turmeric leaves, nutmeg, lemongrass, lime juice and sugar. Mix well, and bring back to a boil. Reduce heat and simmer until mussels open, which is a sign that they are cooked.

4. Season to taste with salt, pepper and lime juice.

5. Garnish as desired.

Kepiting Kuning (Crab in Yellow Turmeric Dressing)
Serves 4

It is best to purchase crabs only on the day they are to be prepared, as crabs do not keep well. When purchasing crabs, make certain they are very active, strong and free of any ammonia smell. Instead of crabs, shellfish like lobsters, prawns or clams also taste delicious when prepared this way.

5 litres heavily salted water
2 kg large mud crabs
2 *salam* leaves
2 kaffir lime leaves, bruised
2 stalks lemongrass, bruised
750 ml *kuah Indonesia* or *kaldu udang* (page 10)
4 tomatoes, peeled, seeded and sliced
2 sour star fruits (carambola), sliced
salt and crushed black pepper, to taste
lime juice, to taste

SPICE PASTE

150 g large red chillies, halved, seeded and sliced
60 g shallots, peeled and sliced
30 g garlic, peeled and sliced
60 g turmeric, peeled and sliced
30 g ginger, peeled and sliced
40 g candlenuts
1 teaspoon roasted and crushed coriander seeds
1 teaspoon roasted dried shrimp paste *(terasi)*
1 tablespoon tamarind pulp, soaked for 15 minutes in 125 ml warm water and strained
4 tablespoons vegetable oil

1. Bring 5 litres of heavily salted water to a boil.

2. Add crabs individually, ensuring water maintains a rapid rolling boil. Boil each crab for 1 minute.

3. Remove crabs and plunge into iced water to prevent crabs from overcooking and set aside to chill for 5 minutes.

4. Drain and dry crabs thoroughly. Break pincers and crush shells evenly with a hammer. Pull off back shell and rinse under running water. Cut into four equal pieces.

5. Prepare spice paste. Combine all ingredients in a stone mortar or food processor and grind into a fine paste.

6. Place into a heavy saucepan with *salam* and kaffir lime leaves and lemongrass. Sauté over medium heat until paste is fragrant and takes on a golden colour.

7. Add crabs and mix well until evenly coated with spice paste.

8. Fill saucepan with *kuah Indonesia* or *kaldu udang* and bring to a boil. Reduce heat and simmer for 1 minute.

9. Add tomatoes and sour star fruits. Mix well and bring to a boil. Season with salt, pepper and a generous squeeze of lime juice.

10. Garnish as desired and serve with *saus pedas tomat* (page 9).

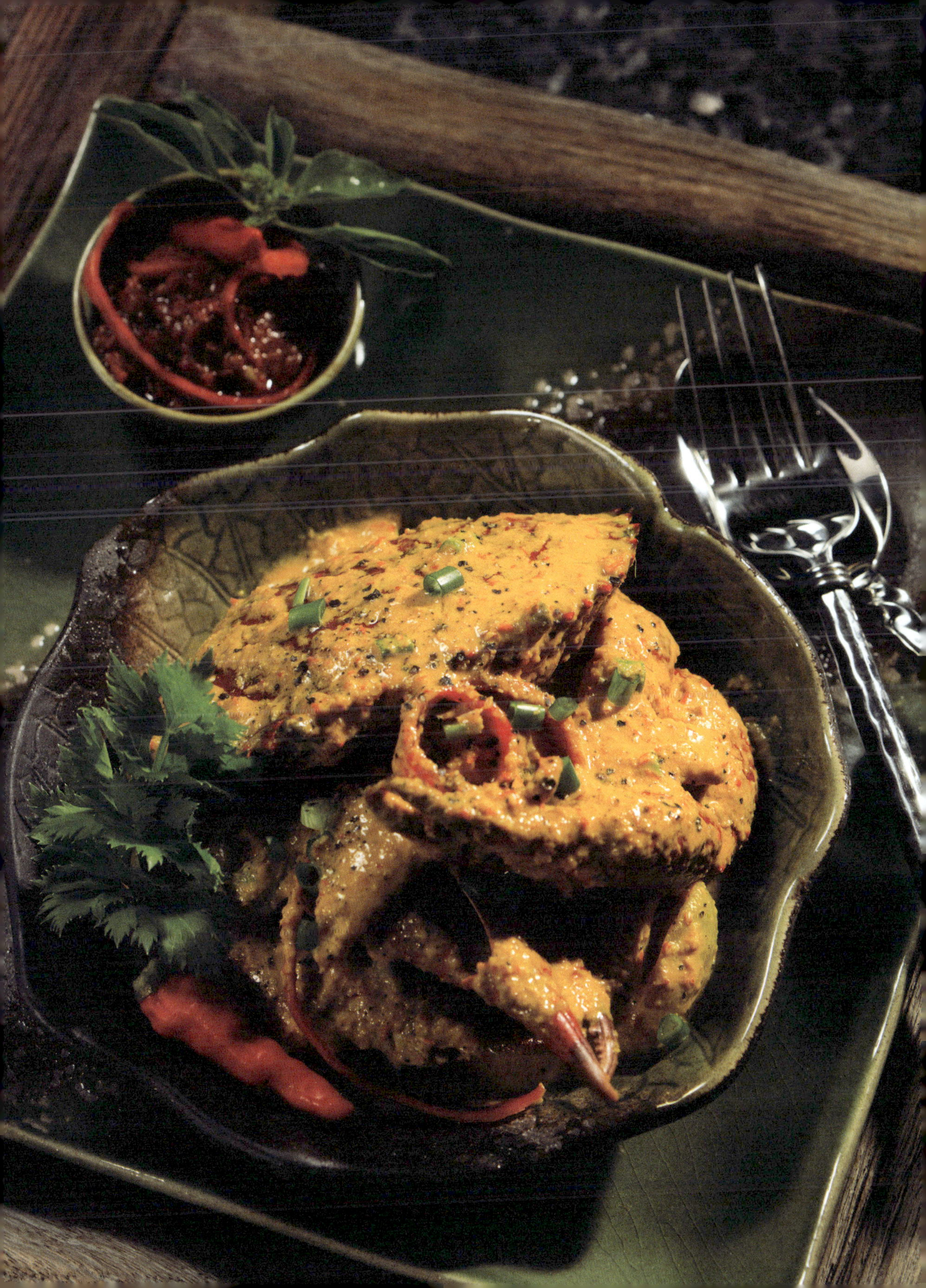

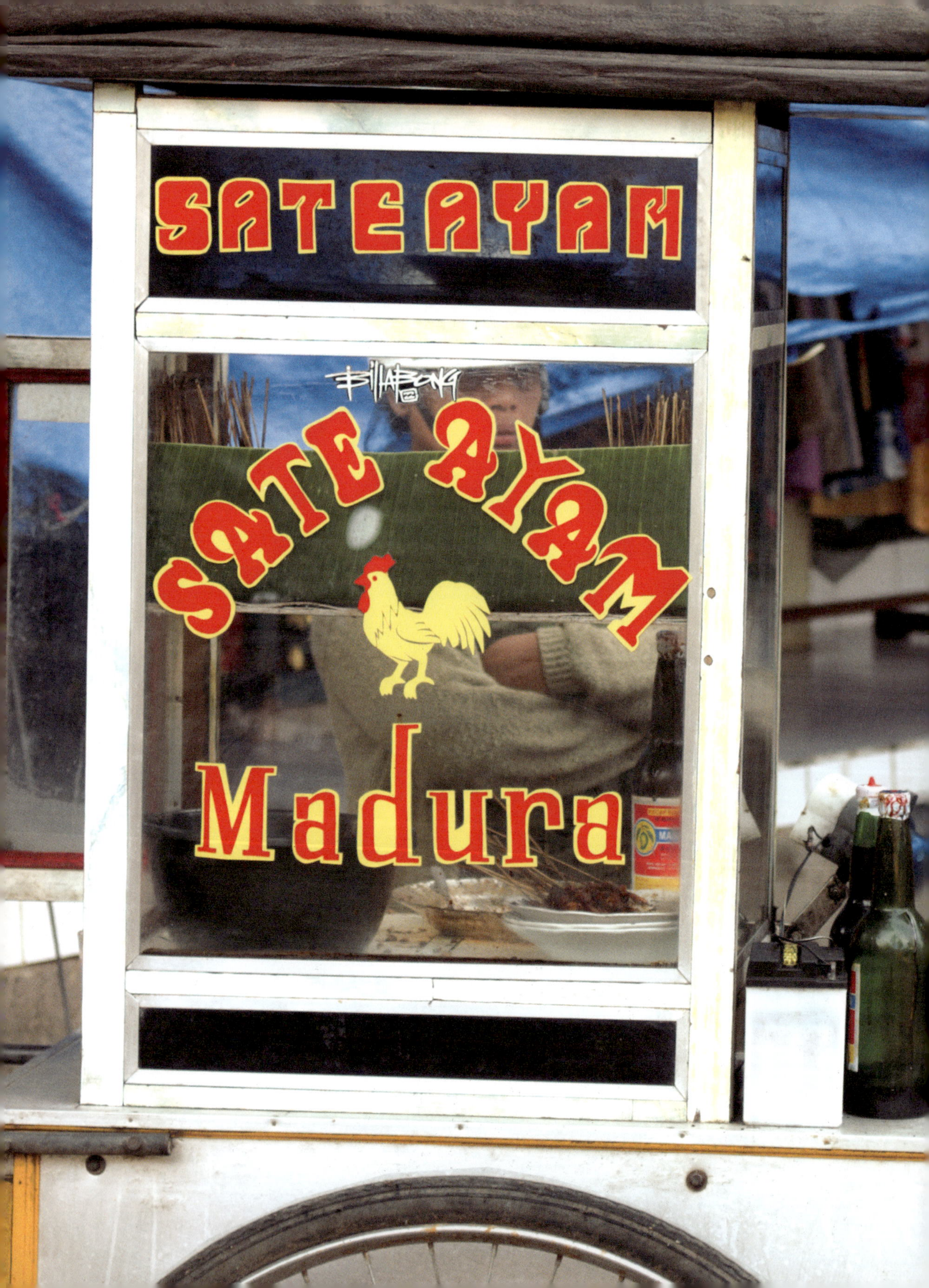
SATE AYAM
SATE AYAM
Madura

Meat & Poultry

Sate Manis (Assorted Satays) 47

Gulai Kambing (Sumatran Lamb Curry) 48

Kaki Kambing
(Lamb Shanks with Cardamom and Cinnamon) 50

Babi Guling (Spit-roasted Small Piglet) 52

Rendang Sapi (Beef Braised with Coconut Milk and Spices) 55

Ayam Taliwang (Grilled Lombok Chicken) 56

Ayam Goreng (Fried Chicken) 59

Opor Ayam (Chicken in Spiced Coconut Sauce) 60

Sate Bebek Lilit (Minced Duck Satay) 62

Bebek Betutu (Roast Duck in Banana Leaf) 65

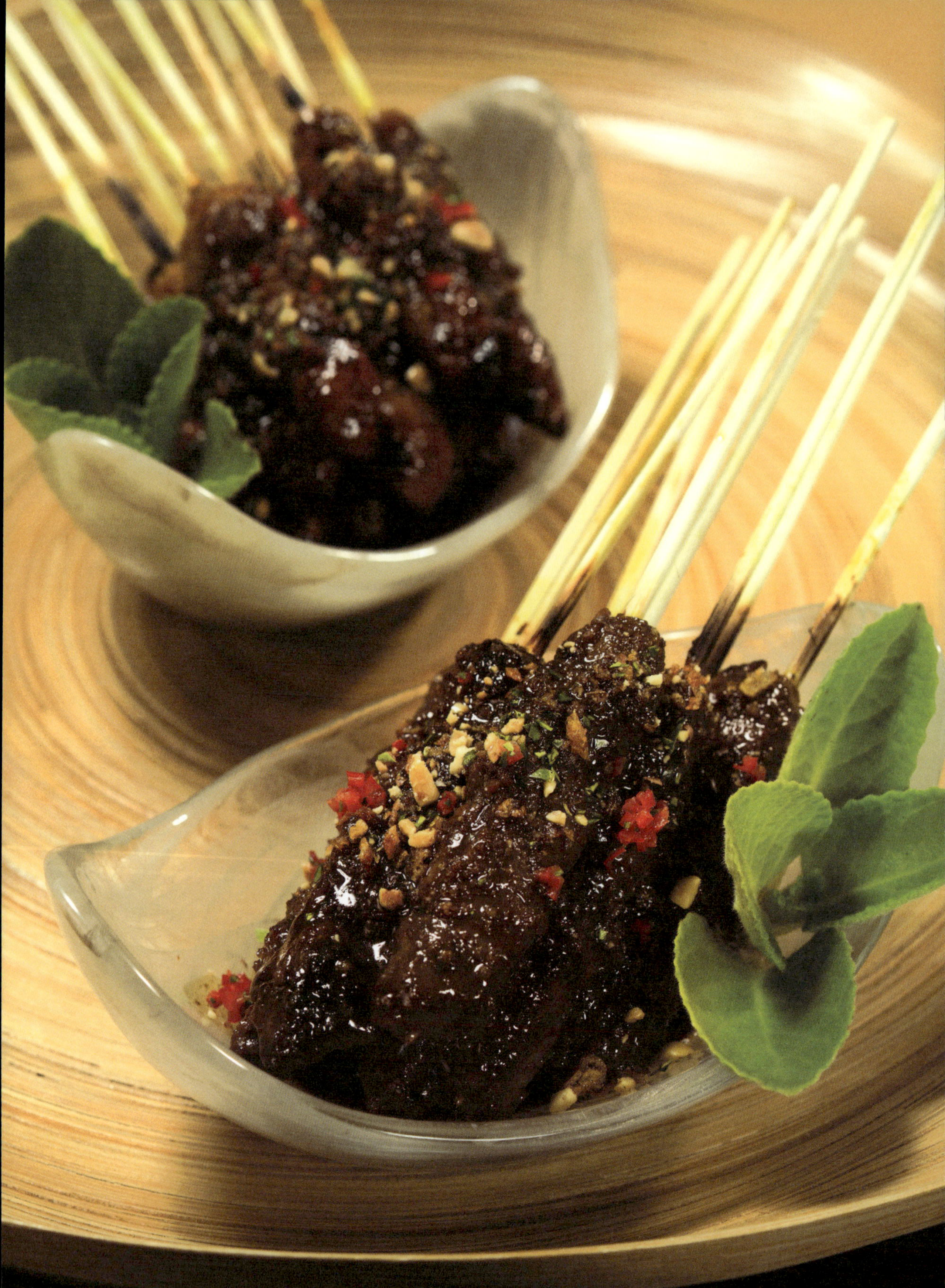

Sate Manis (Assorted Satays) Serves 4–6

Sate is a word that is regularly associated with Indonesian food. Most visitors to Indonesia will probably eat *sate* at their hotel or restaurant lunch stops. These *sates* consist of chunks of meat threaded through a skewer, then grilled to perfection over glowing charcoal.

800 g lamb leg, beef tenderloin, sirloin or topside or boneless skinned chicken leg, cut into 1.5-cm cubes

600 g fermented soybean cakes (*tempeh*), cut into 2-cm cubes

bamboo skewers, as needed, pre-soaked in water

2 limes, cut into wedges

sweet soy sauce *(kecap manis)*, as needed

SPICE PASTE

3 tablespoons coconut oil

60 g shallots, peeled and sliced

40 g garlic, peeled and sliced

70 g large red chillies, halved, seeded and sliced

½ tablespoon roasted and crushed coriander seeds

¼ tablespoon cumin seeds

2 tablespoons lime juice

1 tablespoon chopped palm sugar

¼ tablespoon salt

4 tablespoons sweet soy sauce *(kecap manis)*

1. Prepare spice paste. Combine all ingredients except sweet soy sauce in a stone mortar or food processor and grind into a very fine paste. Add sweet soy sauce and blend well.

2. Combine meat with spice paste, mix well and allow meat to marinate in a cool place for 30 minutes.

3. Thread meat and soybean cakes evenly onto bamboo skewers.

4. Grill over very high heat and serve with lime wedges and sweet soy sauce as a dipping sauce.

A rich creamy *base sate* (page 11) together with rice cakes makes the perfect condiment for these tasty meat skewers.

Gulai Kambing (Sumatran Lamb Curry) Serves 4–6

This dish can also be prepared with chicken, beef, fish or vegetables. For fish, add more ginger and tamarind and less dry spices when preparing the spice blend.

4 tablespoons coconut oil
10-cm cinnamon stick
750 ml *kuah Indonesia* (page 10)
1 stalk lemongrass, bruised
1 turmeric leaf, torn
2 *salam* leaves
2 kaffir lime leaves, torn
½ tablespoon tamarind pulp soaked for 15 minutes in 60 ml water and strained
1.2 kg lamb shoulder, cut into 2.5-cm cubes and brined for 5 hours (1 litre water, 40 g salt and 15 g sugar)
250 ml coconut cream
crushed white peppercorns, to taste
fried shallots, to garnish

FRESH SPICE PASTE
60 g shallots, peeled and sliced
30 g garlic, peeled and sliced
4–6 bird's eye chillies, sliced
30 g ginger, peeled and sliced
30 g galangal *(laos)*, peeled and sliced
30 g turmeric, peeled and sliced

DRY SPICE PASTE
1 teaspoon roasted and crushed coriander seeds
½ teaspoon peeled and crushed cardamom
½ teaspoon crushed caraway seeds
¼ teaspoon ground nutmeg
3 star anise
½ teaspoon crushed white peppercorns

1. Prepare fresh spice paste. Combine all ingredients in a stone mortar or food processor and grind until very fine.

2. Prepare dry spice paste. Combine all ingredients in a different stone mortar or food processor and grind until very fine.

3. Heat oil in heavy saucepan. Add both spice blends and cinnamon stick and sauté over medium heat until spices are fragrant and colour changes.

4. Fill saucepan with *kuah Indonesia*. Add lemongrass, turmeric, *salam* and kaffir lime leaves and tamarind juice and bring to a boil. Reduce heat and simmer for 5 minutes.

5. Add meat and mix well. Return to a boil and reduce heat. Skim off scum.

6. Pressure cook at a gauge pressure of 1 bar /15 psi for 25 minutes. Start timing when full pressure is reached.

7. Let cooker cool for 20 minutes.

8. Lift meat from cooking liquid with a slotted spoon and transfer to a frying pan.

9. Strain liquid into a pot and bring to simmer. Skim off as much fat as possible.

10. Add coconut cream and simmer until sauce is lightly creamy.

11. Transfer sauce to pan with lamb, mix well and simmer over medium heat, gently turning and basting meat until glazed. Simmer for 12–15 minutes until dish turns lightly creamy.

12. Remove pan from heat and let mixture infuse for 7–10 minutes.

13. Season to taste with crushed white peppercorns. Garnish with fried shallots.

If meat takes longer to cook and liquid reduces too much, add small amounts of stock until meat is tender. Do not add more coconut milk as this will make the dish too heavy and oily.

If you prefer a traditional way of preparing this stew, follow steps 1–5 above using a suitable stewing pan. Braise stew in 100°C oven until 90% done. This can take several hours and an exact time is difficult to estimate as it depends on the quality of meat. It is best to stir the stew every 15 minutes and check the doneness of the meat. Follow steps 8–10 to finish cooking the dish.

Yet another delicious way to prepare this dish would be in a crockpot or slow cooker. Follow steps 1–5, then transfer all ingredients into a slow cooker or crockpot and cook at 70°C for 8 hours or until meat is 90% soft. Once again, the quality of the meat would determine the exact timing. Follow steps 8–10 to finish cooking the dish.

Kaki Kambing (Lamb Shanks with Cardamom and Cinnamon) Serves 4

Mutton is principally used in Javanese owned restaurants to make a popular *sate*, as well as dishes such as *gulai* and *kare*. The Balinese also adore lamb *sate* and other mutton dishes such as this one.

4 tablespoons coconut oil
2 stalks lemongrass, bruised
4 kaffir lime leaves, bruised
10-cm cinnamon stick
4 lamb shanks, each about 350 g
500 ml *kuah Indonesia* (page 10)
250 ml coconut cream
salt, to taste
2 tablespoons lime juice and lime zest
celery leaves, diced tomatoes, fried shallots and leek, to garnish

SPICE BLEND

1 tablespoon roasted and crushed coriander seeds
½ tablespoon peeled and crushed cardamom
½ teaspoon cumin
¼ teaspoon ground nutmeg
4 cloves, crushed
½ teaspoon crushed black peppercorns

SPICE PASTE

60 g shallots, peeled and sliced
40 g garlic, peeled and sliced
75 g large red chillies, halved, seeded and sliced
30g turmeric, peeled and sliced
30 g ginger, peeled and sliced
30 g galangal *(laos)*, peeled and sliced
3 tablespoons tamarind pulp dissolved in 60 ml warm water and strained

1. Prepare spice blend. Combine all ingredients in a frying pan and dry-fry until fragrant.

2. Prepare spice paste. Combine roasted spices and ingredients for spice paste in a stone mortar or food processor and grind into a fine paste.

3. Heat oil in a heavy saucepan. Add spice paste, lemongrass, kaffir lime leaves and cinnamon stick. Sauté over medium heat until spices are fragrant and the colour changes.

4. Add lamb shanks and continue to sauté until meat is evenly coated and golden.

5. Fill saucepan with *kuah Indonesia*, blend well and bring to a simmer.

6. Transfer to a pressure cooker and bring back to a simmer. Skim off scum.

7. Pressure cook at a gage pressure of 1 bar / 15 psi for 40–45 minutes. Start timing once full pressure is reached.

8. Turn off heat and allow cooker to cool for 30 minutes.

9. Strain two-thirds of liquid into a saucepan and bring to a quick boil. Remove scum and reduce heat.

10. Add coconut cream, bring back to a boil and simmer for 3 minutes. Add lamb shanks and remaining sauce and simmer over medium low heat for 12–15 minutes, until shanks are glazed and sauce is lightly creamy. Remove from heat, and let mixture infuse for 7–10 minutes.

11. With a hand blender, quickly foam up sauce.

12. Season sauce to taste with salt, 2 tablespoons lime juice and lime zest.

13. Garnish dish with celery leaves, diced tomatoes, fried shallots and leek.

If you prefer a more traditional approach, follow steps 1–5 above using a cast-iron or heavy stew pan. Braise lamb shanks in 100°C oven. Check every 15 minutes for doneness and also to give the dish a good mix. This will take several hours depending on the quality of the meat. Follow steps 9–13 to finish cooking the dish.

Babi Guling (Spit-roasted Small Piglet) Serves 14–16

The word "*guling*" is best translated into English as "rotated", or in the case of cooking, "rotisserie". Basically this dish is a cleaned pig stuffed with spices and roasted over coals or a low fire, which often takes hours. This dish is popularly served in restaurants throughout Bali.

- 1 small piglet, weighing 8–10 kg, thoroughly cleaned
- 2 tablespoons salt
- 800 g cassava leaves, cleaned, blanched for 5 minutes and roughly sliced, or spinach leaves
- 200 g shallots, peeled and sliced
- 100 g garlic, peeled and sliced
- 100 g ginger, peeled and chopped
- 200 g turmeric, peeled and chopped
- 100 g galangal *(laos)*, peeled and finely chopped
- 75 g candlenuts, chopped
- 100 g bird's eye chillies, finely sliced
- 10 stalks lemongrass, bruised, finely sliced and chopped
- 3 tablespoons crushed coriander seeds
- 1 tablespoon crushed black peppercorns
- 2 tablespoons roasted and crumbled dried shrimp paste (*terasi*)
- 5 kaffir lime leaves, finely chopped
- 2 *salam* leaves
- vegetable oil for basting
- 250 ml turmeric water, made by blending 100 g freshly ground turmeric with 200 ml water

1. Season piglet well with salt.

2. Combine all other ingredients, except turmeric water and mix thoroughly.

3. Stuff pig with mixture, then close belly with string or *sate* skewers.

4. Brush outside of piglet with turmeric water until skin is shiny and yellow.

5. Preheat oven to 120°C and roast piglet for about 3 hours. Let rest for 45 minutes in a warm place.

6. Approximately 30 minutes before serving, heat oven to its highest possible temperature (which should be between 250°C and 275°C) and roast piglet for 10–20 minutes. This process will make the skin really crispy.

7. When serving, first remove the crispy skin with a carving knife or a pair of scissors. Loosen meat from bones and cut into even slices. Serve with stuffing and steamed rice.

If you have a large barbecue with a rotisserie or turning spit, you can cook the pig over burning charcoal for an authentic Balinese flavour. To roast this delicate pig to perfection, insert a meat thermometer into the thickest part of the leg and slowly roast until the temperature reaches 71°C.

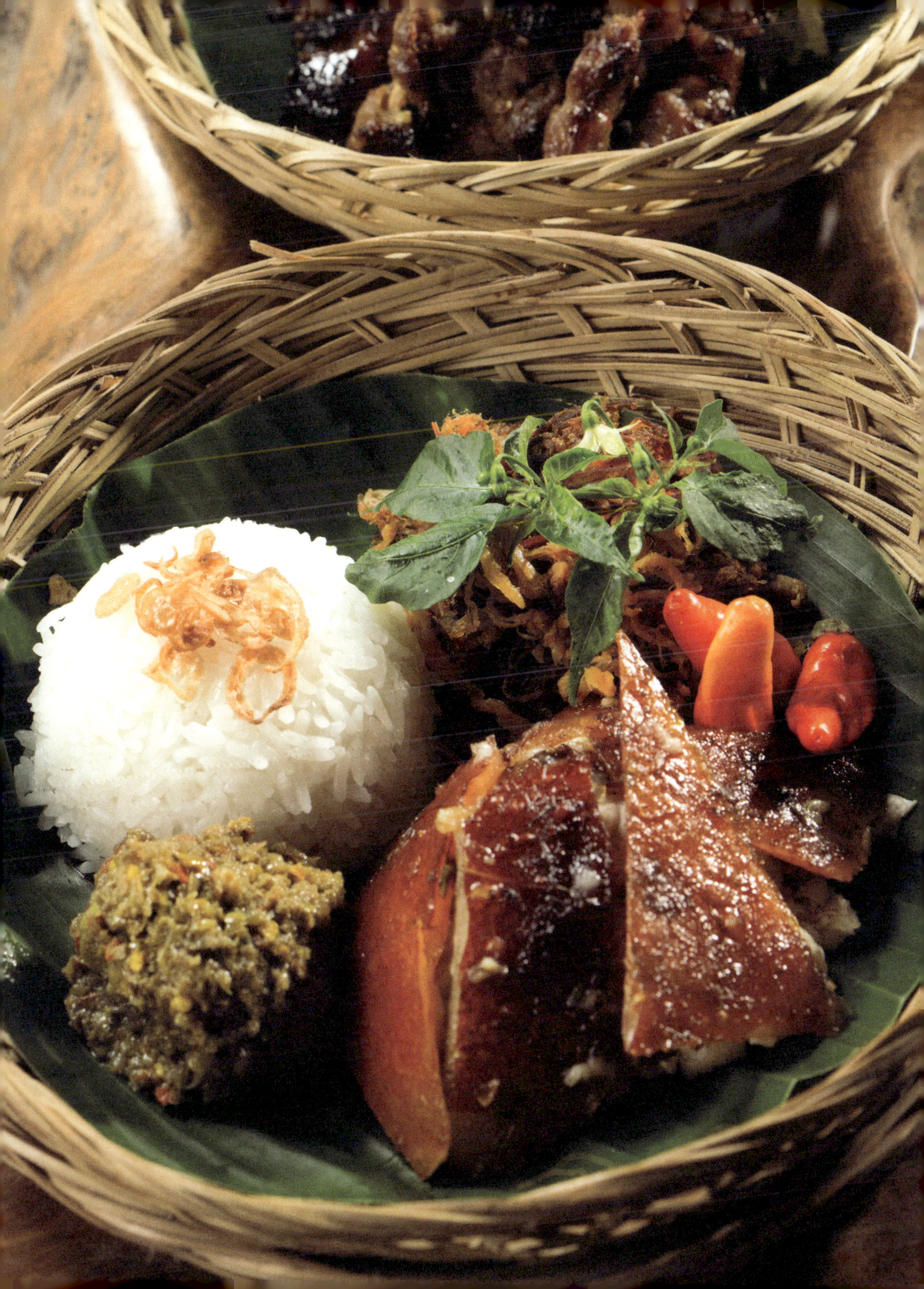

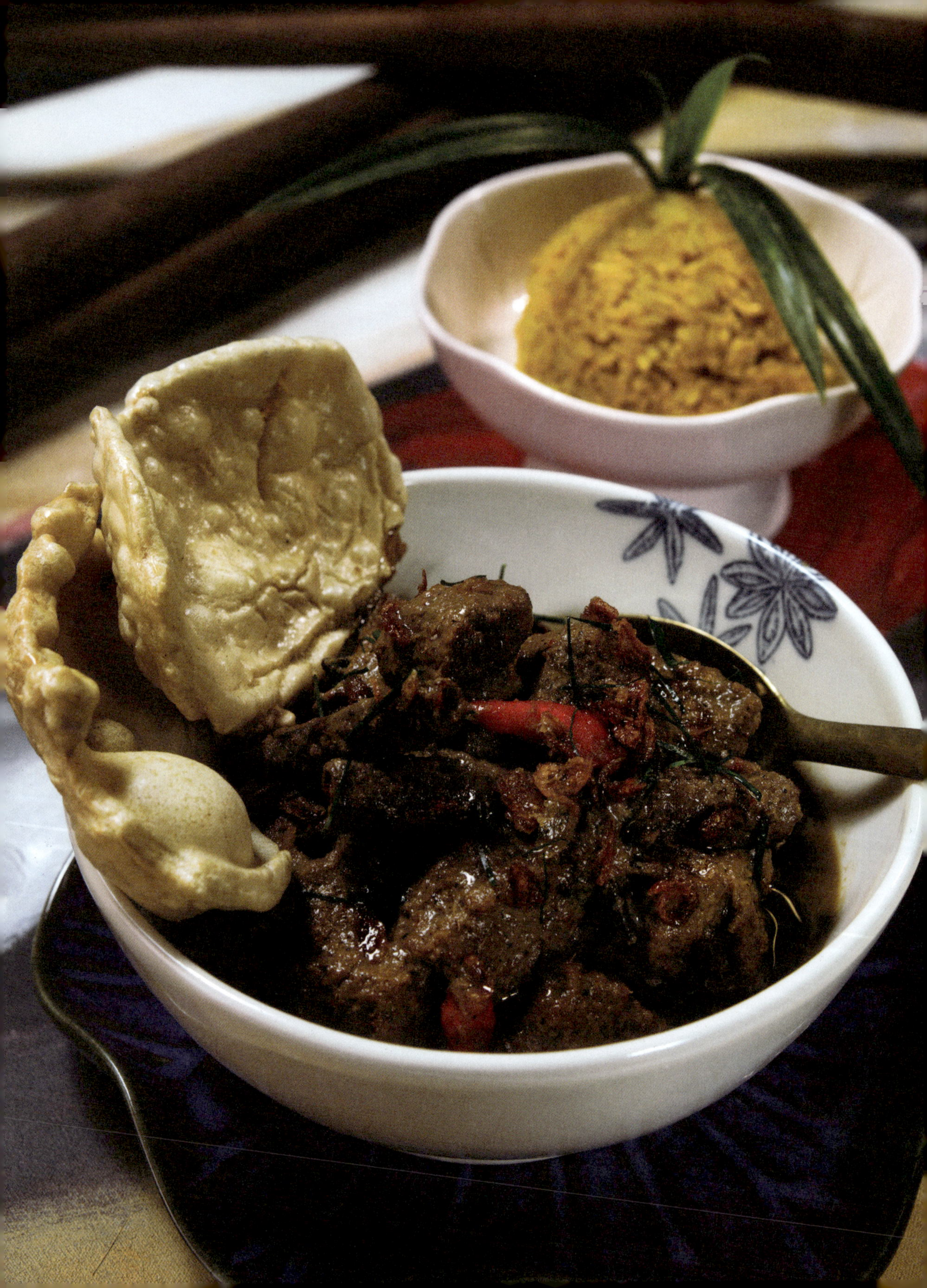

Rendang Sapi (Beef Braised with Coconut Milk and Spices) Serves 4

To learn how to prepare this imperial dish, I flew 4 hours across Indonesia to Padang where Pak Dian, a talented and very passionate young chef introduced me to all the secrets of this incredible tasty beef dish. It took him two full days to go through the process before I had the joy of indulging in this creamy stew.

- 3 tablespoons coconut oil
- 2.4 litres coconut milk
- 3 stalks lemongrass, bruised
- 4 *salam* leaves
- 1 turmeric leaf, torn and knotted (If not available, replace with 30 g fresh peeled turmeric which you can add to the spice paste)
- 4 kaffir lime leaves, bruised
- 7-cm cinnamon stick
- 1.2 kg beef shoulder or neck, cut into 2.5-cm cubes and brined for 5 hours
- salt, to taste

DRY SPICES

- 1 tablespoon coriander seeds
- 1 teaspoon cardamom seeds
- ¼ teaspoon crushed nutmeg
- 8 cloves
- ½ teaspoon ground white pepper

SPICE PASTE

- 80 g shallots, peeled and sliced
- 50 g garlic, peeled and sliced
- 120 g large red chillies, halved, seeded and sliced
- 5–7 bird's eye chillies, sliced
- 50 g galangal *(laos)*, peeled and sliced
- 50 g ginger, peeled and sliced
- 50 g candlenuts, roasted and crushed

1. Prepare dry spices. Combine all ingredients in a stone mortar and grind until very fine. Set aside.

2. Prepare spice paste. Combine all ingredients in a stone mortar or food processor and grind into a fine paste.

3. Heat coconut oil in heavy saucepan, add spice paste and sauté over medium heat until fragrant and colour changes. Add ground dry spices.

4. Add coconut milk and blend well. Add lemongrass, *salam*, turmeric and kaffir lime leaves and cinnamon. Simmer over medium heat for about 1 hour until coconut milk is oily and paste is creamy and dark brown in colour.

5. Add beef cubes and bring to a boil. Reduce heat and simmer until meat is tender, stirring frequently until liquid has almost evaporated and dish looks dry and oily. There should be almost no liquid left when cooked. Season to taste with salt.

6. Garnish as desired. Serve with *nasi kuning* (page 15).

Ayam Taliwang (Grilled Lombok Chicken) Serves 4–6

This simply marinated chicken is usually deep-fried, but I find that it tastes just as good when grilled, and is certainly a healthier choice.

2 stalks lemongrass, bruised
4 *salam* leaves
3 kaffir lime leaves
750 ml *kuah Indonesia* (page 10)
250 ml coconut cream
salt, to taste
1 tablespoon lime juice
4 spring chickens, 800 g each, opened butterfly-style and completely deboned
coconut or vegetable oil, as needed

SPICE PASTE
3 tablespoons coconut oil
1/4 teaspoon ground black pepper
5–7 bird's eye chillies, sliced
70 g large red chillies, halved, seeded and sliced
70 g shallots, peeled and sliced
50 g garlic, peeled and sliced
40 g ginger, peeled and sliced
40 g galangal *(laos)*, peeled and sliced
40 g turmeric, peeled and sliced
1 teaspoon palm sugar
1 teaspoon roasted shrimp paste *(terasi)*

1. Prepare spice paste. Combine all ingredients in a stone mortar or food processor and grind into a fine paste. Transfer spice pastes into a heavy saucepan. Add lemongrass, *salam* and kaffir lime leaves and slowly heat until spices are fragrant and soft. Reserve one-quarter cup of spice paste for basting.

2. Fill saucepan with *kuah Indonesia*, bring to a boil and simmer for 10 minutes. Add coconut cream and bring back to a simmer. Allow sauce to cool. Season to taste with salt and lime juice.

3. Place each chicken into a vacuum bag. Add 100 ml of sauce and vacuum seal the bags.

4. Vacuum cook chicken or cook in a ziplock bag at 65°C for 50 minutes. Remove chicken from cooking liquid and place on a rack and let rest for 45 minutes. This will allow the skin to dry and turn golden crispy when grilled.

5. Bring cooking liquid back to a boil and reduce until sauce thickens and coconut cream starts to break down. This makes a delicious dipping sauce.

6. Combine reserved spice paste with an equal amount of coconut or vegetable oil. Evenly brush chicken pieces with this marinade.

7. Grill chicken over very hot glowing charcoal until golden brown. Baste frequently with basting mix on both sides to prevent chicken from burning and to give chicken a golden, shiny colour.

8. Serve with dipping sauce and *saus pedas tomat* (page 9).

Alternatively, you can also cook the chicken in a slow cooker or crockpot. Follow steps 1–2 above, then add chickens to sauce, bring sauce back to a simmer, and blend well. Transfer chicken and sauce into slow cooker or crockpot set at 68°C–70°C and simmer for 2 hours. Follow steps 3–8 to finish cooking the dish.

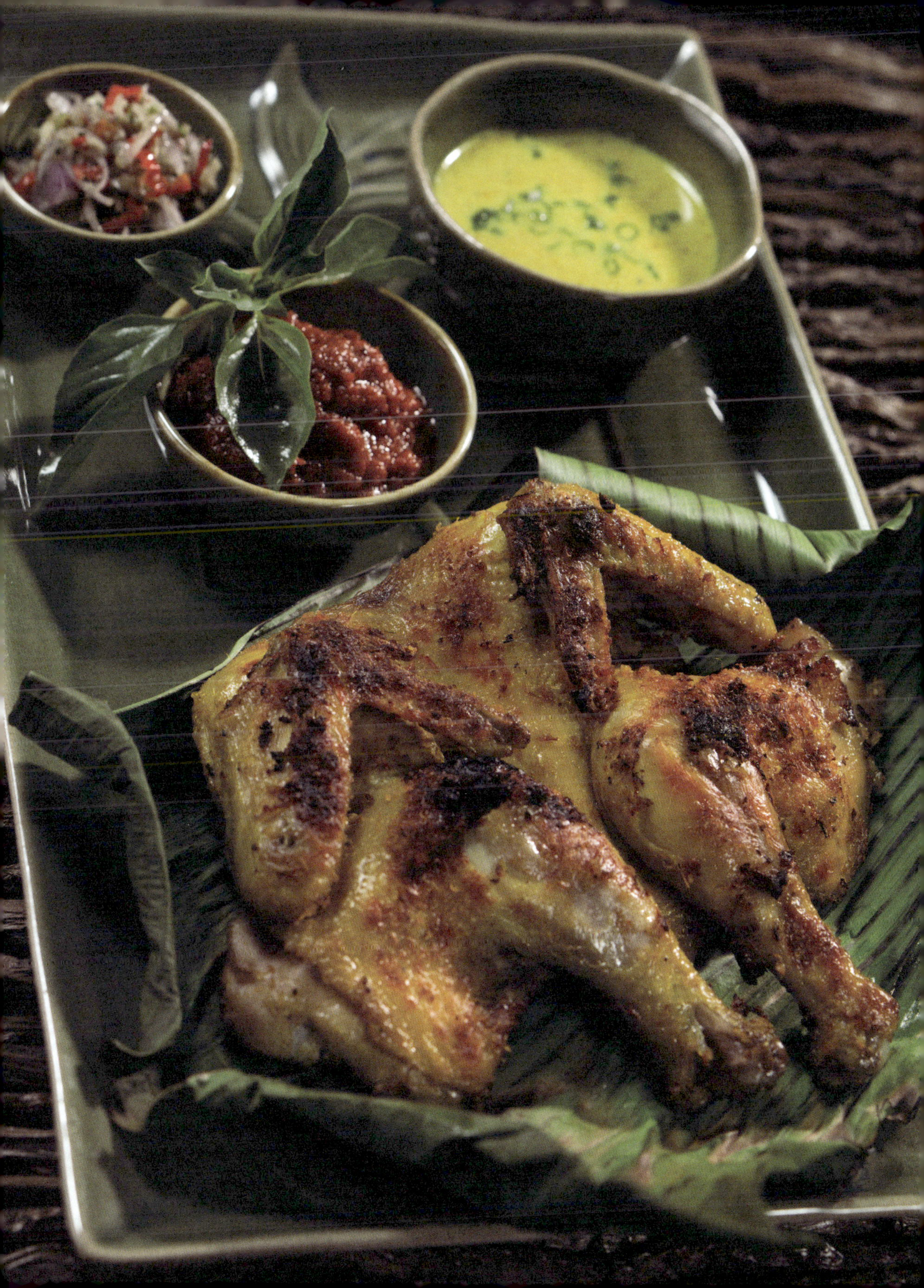

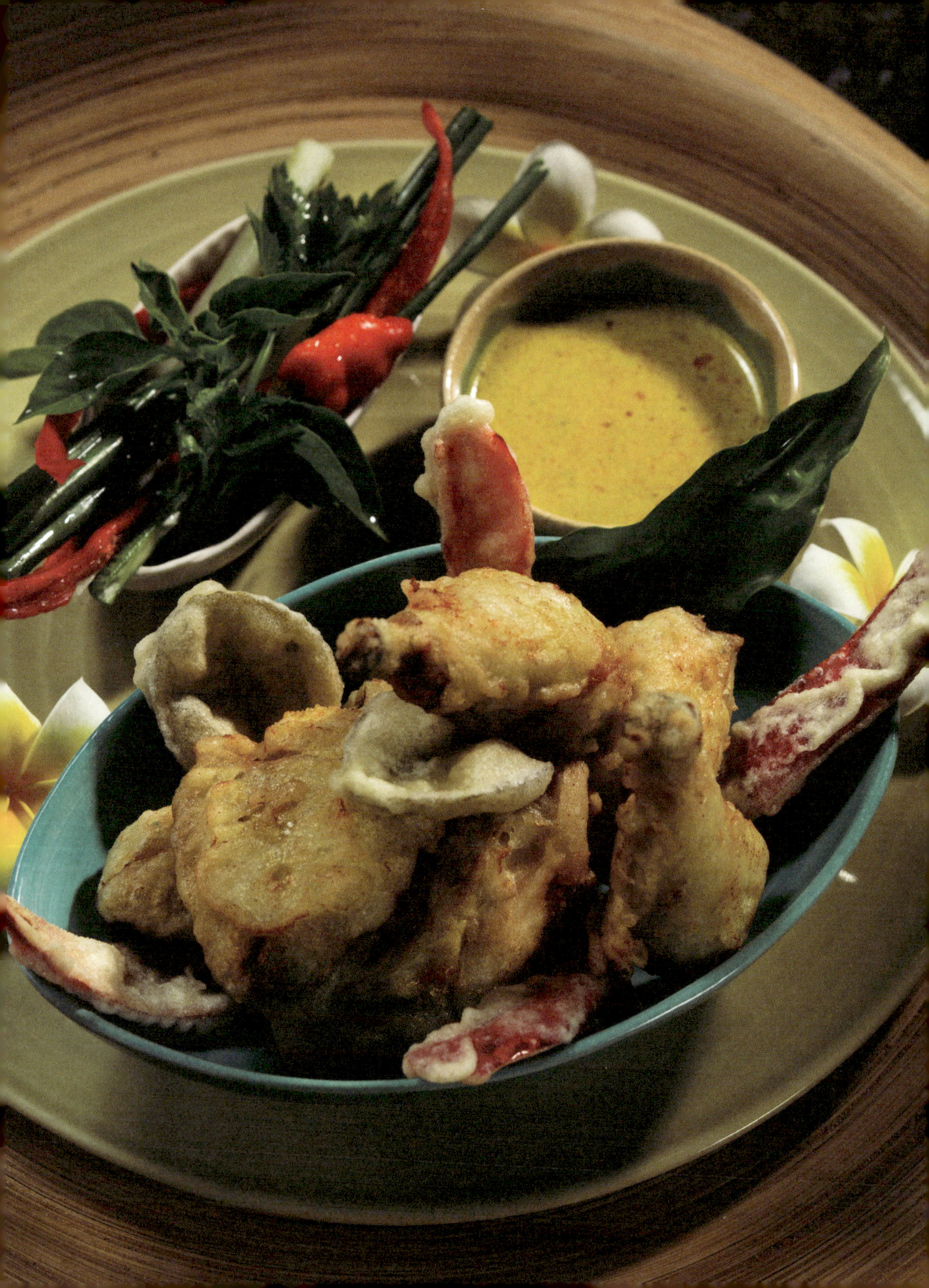

Ayam Goreng (Fried Chicken) Serves 4–6

It's amazing how a simple seasoning of salt and turmeric brings out the flavour of the chicken in this basic recipe.

2 stalks lemongrass, bruised
4 *salam* leaves
3 kaffir lime leaves
750 ml *kuah Indonesia* (page 10)
250 ml coconut cream
salt, to taste
1 tablespoon lime juice
4 spring chickens, 800 g each, opened butterfly-style and completely deboned
coconut or vegetable oil, as needed
4 tablespoons rice flour
coconut or vegetable oil, for frying

SPICE PASTE
3 tablespoons coconut oil
1/4 teaspoon black pepper
5–7 bird's eye chillies, sliced
70 g large red chillies, halved, seeded and sliced
70 g shallots, peeled and sliced
50 g garlic, peeled and sliced
40 g ginger, peeled and sliced
40 g galangal *(laos)*, peeled and sliced
40 g turmeric, peeled and sliced
1 teaspoon palm sugar
1 teaspoon roasted dried shrimp paste *(terasi)*

1. Prepare spice paste. Combine ingredients in a stone mortar or food processor and grind into a fine paste. Transfer ground spices to a heavy saucepan. Add lemongrass, salam and kaffir lime leaves and slowly heat until spices are fragrant and soft. Reserve one-quarter cup of spice paste for basting.

2. Fill saucepan with *kuah Indonesia*, bring to a boil and simmer for 10 minutes. Add coconut cream and bring back to a simmer. Allow sauce to cool. Season to taste with salt and lime juice.

3. Vacuum cook chicken or cook in a ziplock bag at 65°C for 50 minutes. Remove chicken from cooking liquid and place on a rack and let rest for 45 minutes.

4. Bring cooking liquid back to a boil and reduce until sauce thickens and coconut cream starts to break down. This makes a delicious dipping sauce.

5. Combine reserved spice paste with an equal amount of coconut or vegetable oil. Evenly brush chicken pieces with this marinade.

6. Dust chicken evenly with rice flour and deep-fry over high heat (180°C) for 2 minutes until golden brown. Drain on kitchen towels.

7. Serve with dipping sauce.

Alternatively, you can also prepare this dish with a slow cooker or crockpot. Follow steps 1–2 above, then add chickens to sauce and bring sauce back to simmer, blend well. Then transfer chicken and sauce into slow cooker or crockpot set at 68°C–70°C and simmer for 2 hours. Follow steps 3–8 to finish cooking the dish.

Opor Ayam (Chicken in Spiced Coconut Sauce) Serves 4–6

This has to be one of Central Java's most popular dishes prepared on a daily basis in everyone's home. Most ceremonies and royal banquets would not be complete without *opor ayam* as well. This version is a little more labour intensive and takes a longer time to prepare but the gentle cooking will result in an incredibly tasty dish.

4 baby chickens, 750 g each, opened butterfly-style and completely deboned

100 ml vegetable or coconut oil

15 g palm sugar, chopped

375 ml *kuah Indonesia* (page 10)

125 ml coconut cream

3 stalks lemongrass, bruised

2 *salam* leaves

3 kaffir lime leaves, bruised

1 pinch salt + more to taste

lime zest and lime juice, to taste

4 chicken eggs or 20 quail eggs

200 g potatoes, peeled and cut into even pieces

1 stalk young leek, finely sliced

fried shallots and finely sliced red chillies, to garnish

BRINE

1 litre water

40 g salt

15 g sugar

SPICE BLEND

1 tablespoon roasted coriander seeds

1 teaspoon roasted cumin

$1/2$ teaspoon crushed white peppercorns

2 tablespoons coconut oil

30 g galangal *(laos)*, peeled and sliced

60 g shallots, peeled and sliced

30 g garlic, peeled and sliced

30 g candlenuts, roasted and crushed

1. Brine chickens in water, salt and sugar for 5 hours. Refrigerate for first 3 hours before setting aside at room temperature for remaining 2 hours. Rinse chickens thoroughly under running water and pat dry with kitchen towels.

2. Heat oil until smoking. Quickly sear each chicken for 30 seconds on each side until light golden. Set aside and allow oil to drain and chicken to cool.

3. Prepare spice blend. Combine coriander seeds, cumin and white peppercorns in a stone mortar or food processor and grind finely. Add all other ingredients and grind into a fine paste.

4. Heat 2 tablespoons oil in a heavy saucepan. Add spice paste and palm sugar and sauté until fragrant. Fill saucepan with *kuah Indonesia* and coconut cream. Add lemongrass, *salam* and kaffir lime leaves. Bring to a boil, then reduce heat and simmer for 5 minutes. Season to taste with a small pinch of salt. Add chicken and poach for 40 minutes at 75°C.

5. Alternatively, place chicken individually into heatproof plastic bags. Fill bags with equal amounts of cooled sauce. Make certain not to wet the area of the bag that will be sealed. Vacuum seal and cook at 65°C for 40 minutes Open bags and remove chicken. Set aside.

6. Pour sauce into a saucepan and bring to a simmer. Season with salt, lime zest and lime juice. Using a hand blender, blend sauce for 15 seconds.

7. Place eggs in a small pot of warm water. Cover and quickly bring to a boil. When water comes to a boil, remove pot from heat. Cover with lid and wait for 3 minutes. Drain water and plunge eggs into iced water for 10 seconds. Do not allow eggs to cool. Peel eggs and add to coconut sauce.

8. Place potatoes into a saucepan, fill with warm water and add a generous pinch of salt. Boil potatoes until tender.

9. Cut chickens into halves and arrange on a serving dish. Serve with eggs and potatoes. Pour sauce over and garnish with finely sliced young leek, fried shallots and finely sliced red chillies.

Should sauce be too thick, add small amounts of chicken stock. Serve with steamed rice or rice cakes.

Sate Bebek Lilit (Minced Duck Satay) Serves 4

This is perhaps Bali's most original sate made from pounded meat that is then wrapped around a flattened skewer. Making sate lembat is time-consuming because of the care with which the meat must be prepared and also the delicate task of wrapping the meat around the sticks, but the taste is immensely rewarding!

3 tablespoons coconut oil
400 g minced duck meat (leg meat would be preferred)
200 g minced pork shoulder
125 g grated coconut
4 bird's eye chillies, finely chopped
2 tablespoons fried shallots
1 tablespoon fried garlic
1 teaspoon finely chopped palm sugar
salt, to taste
1 pinch crushed black peppercorns
bamboo skewers or trimmed lemongrass stalks

SPICE PASTE

60 g large red chillies, halved, seeded and sliced
60 g shallots, peeled and sliced
30 g garlic, peeled
20 g galangal *(laos)*, peeled and sliced
30 g turmeric, peeled and sliced
20 g ginger, peeled and sliced
20 g candlenuts, crushed
¼ teaspoon roasted dry shrimp paste (*terasi*)
¼ teaspoon crushed coriander seeds
1 pinch crushed black peppercorns
1 pinch ground nutmeg
2 cloves

1. Prepare spice paste. Combine all ingredients in a stone mortar or food processor and grind into a fine paste.

2. Heat oil in heavy saucepan. Add ground spices and sauté over low heat until fragrant and colour changes. Set aside to cool.

3. Combine minced duck and minced pork with grated coconut, 4 tablespoons spice paste, bird's eye chillies, fried shallots, fried garlic, palm sugar, salt and peppercorns and mix well into a smooth paste.

4. Mould one heaped tablespoonful of this mixture around a wooden skewer or over the trimmed bulbous end of a lemongrass stalk.

5. Grill over very hot charcoal until golden brown, basting frequently with a basting mix made from 2 tablespoons of remaining spice paste and 2 tablespoons vegetable oil.

6. Serve with compressed rice cakes and a creamy *base sate* (page 11).

Duck meat can also be replaced with pork or chicken.

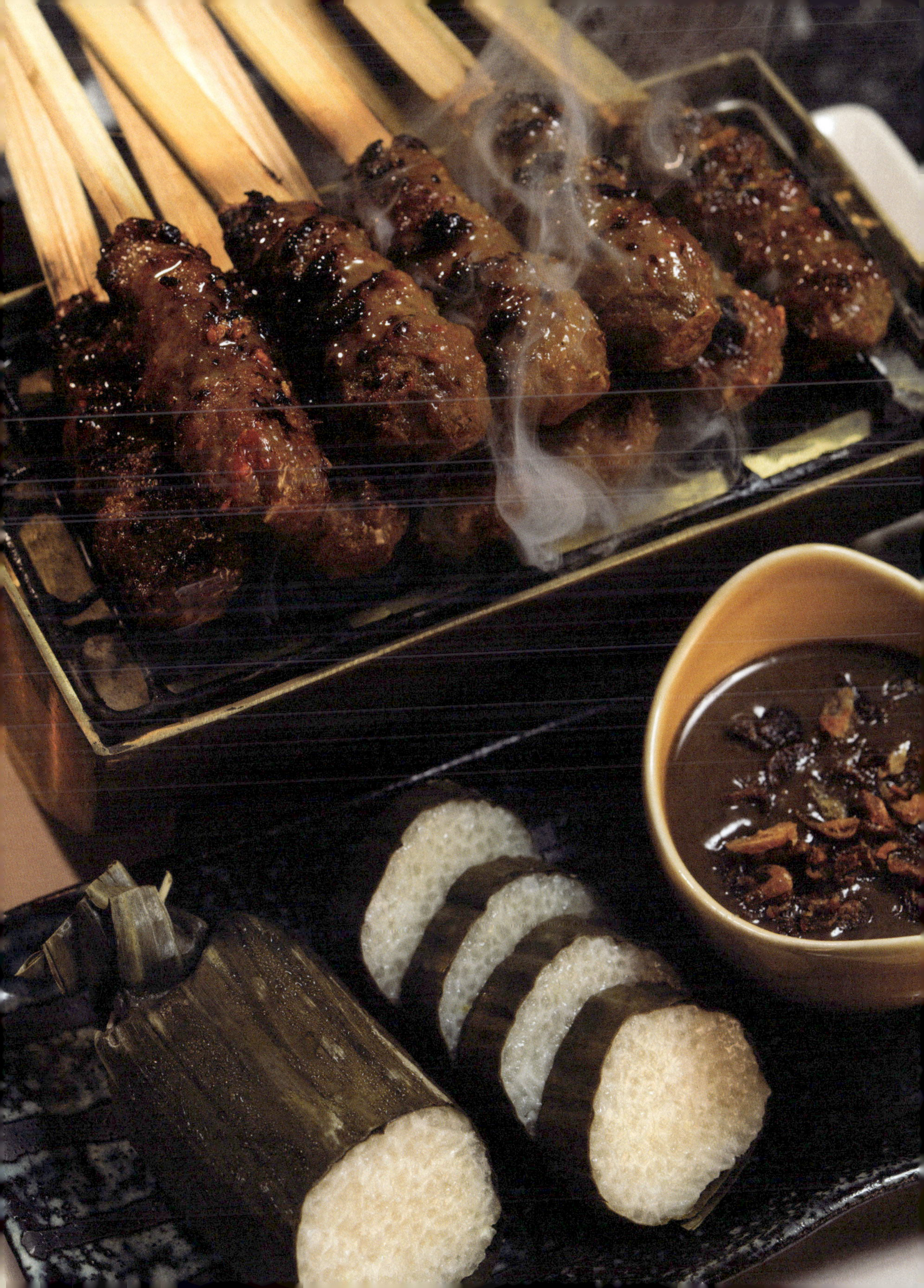

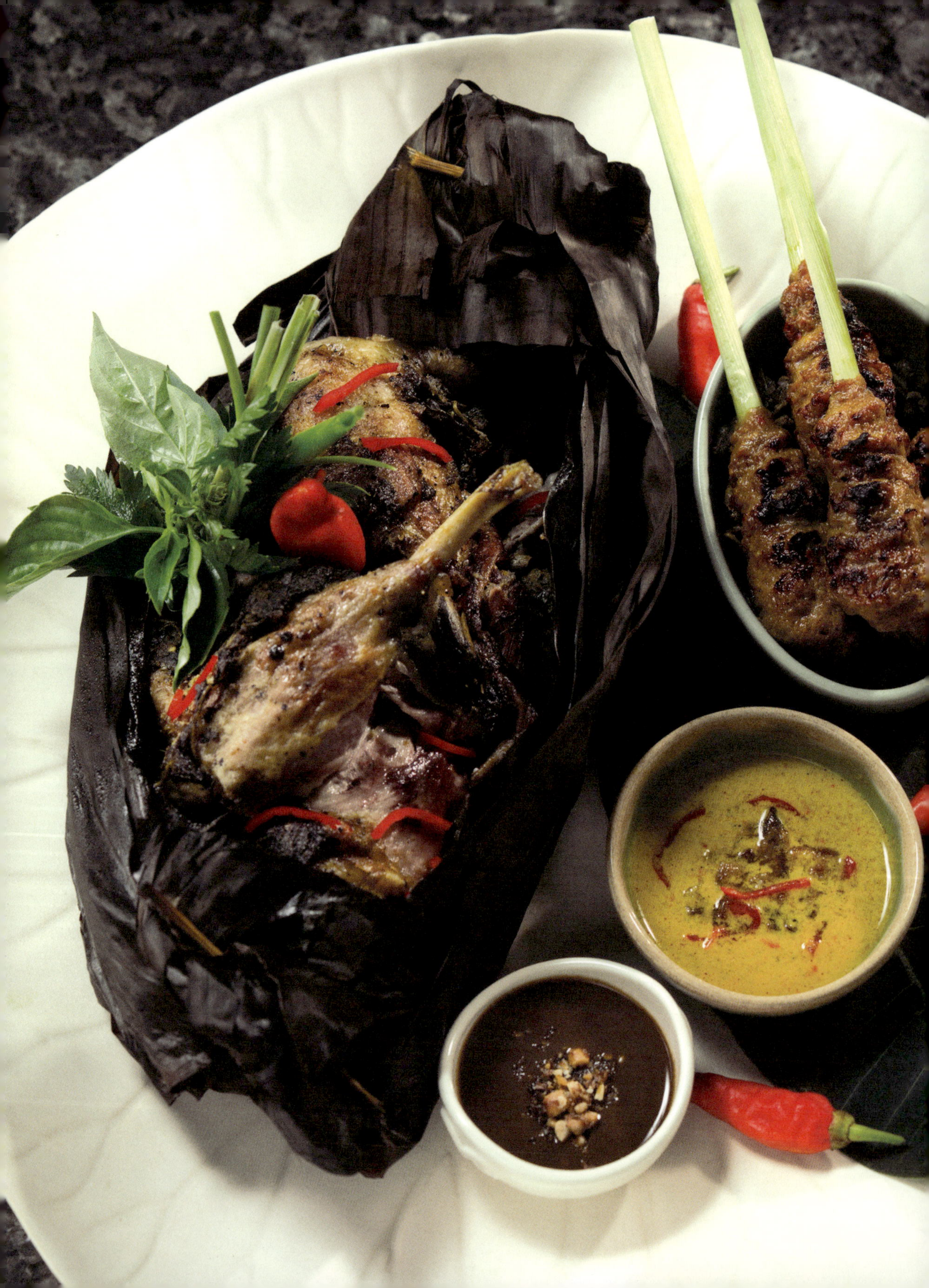

Bebek Betutu (Roast Duck in Banana Leaf) Serves 4–6

The rich flavour of duck is greatly enhanced by the host of pungent roots, herbs and seasoning used in this dish, which is invariably a great favourite with tourists. The Balinese have great admiration for the duck and consider it to be a particularly strong animal as it is one of the few animals able to survive on land as on water.

1 whole duck, weighing about 2 kg

salt and crushed black pepper, to taste

200 g cassava leaves, blanched for 3 minutes and roughly chopped, or spinach leaves, blanched for 15 seconds

4 *salam* leaves

sate skewers, as needed

banana leaves, greaseproof paper or aluminium foil for wrapping

BRINE

1 litre water

45 g salt

15 g sugar

STUFFING

70 g shallots, peeled, halved and sliced

30 g garlic, peeled, halved, and sliced

40 g ginger, peeled and sliced

40 g turmeric, peeled and sliced

25 g lesser galangal *(kencur)*, peeled and sliced

30 g galangal *(laos)*, peeled and sliced

30 g crushed candlenuts

4–7 bird's eye chillies, sliced

1 teaspoon crushed black peppercorns

1 teaspoon crushed coriander seeds

2 teaspoons coarsely crushed roasted dried shrimp paste *(terasi)*

3 stalks lemongrass, finely sliced

5 kaffir lime leaves, finely chopped

salt, to taste

3 tablespoons coconut oil

1. Wash duck thoroughly and pat dry. Brine duck in water, salt and sugar for 12 hours.

2. Remove duck from brine and rinse thoroughly under warm running water. Dry duck well.

3. Season duck with very little salt and crushed black pepper.

4. Prepare stuffing. Combine all ingredients except oil in a stone mortar or food processor and grind into a fine paste. Spoon one-third of paste into a separate bowl and add 3 tablespoons coconut oil. Mix well. Set aside for brushing duck.

5. Combine cassava and *salam* leaves with remaining two-thirds of stuffing and spoon into cavity of duck. Seal duck with a *sate* skewer.

6. Brush outside of duck with stuffing-coconut oil mixture.

7. Wrap duck in several layers of banana leaves and secure with *sate* skewers, or use greaseproof paper or aluminium foil if banana leaves are unavailable.

8. Steam duck over medium heat until a meat thermometer inserted into the meat reads 65°C.

9. Remove top layer of wrapping and bake duck at 220°C for 15 minutes, or until golden brown. When done, the meat should be so tender that it falls off the bones.

10. Unwrap duck and cut into small pieces. Serve with stuffing.

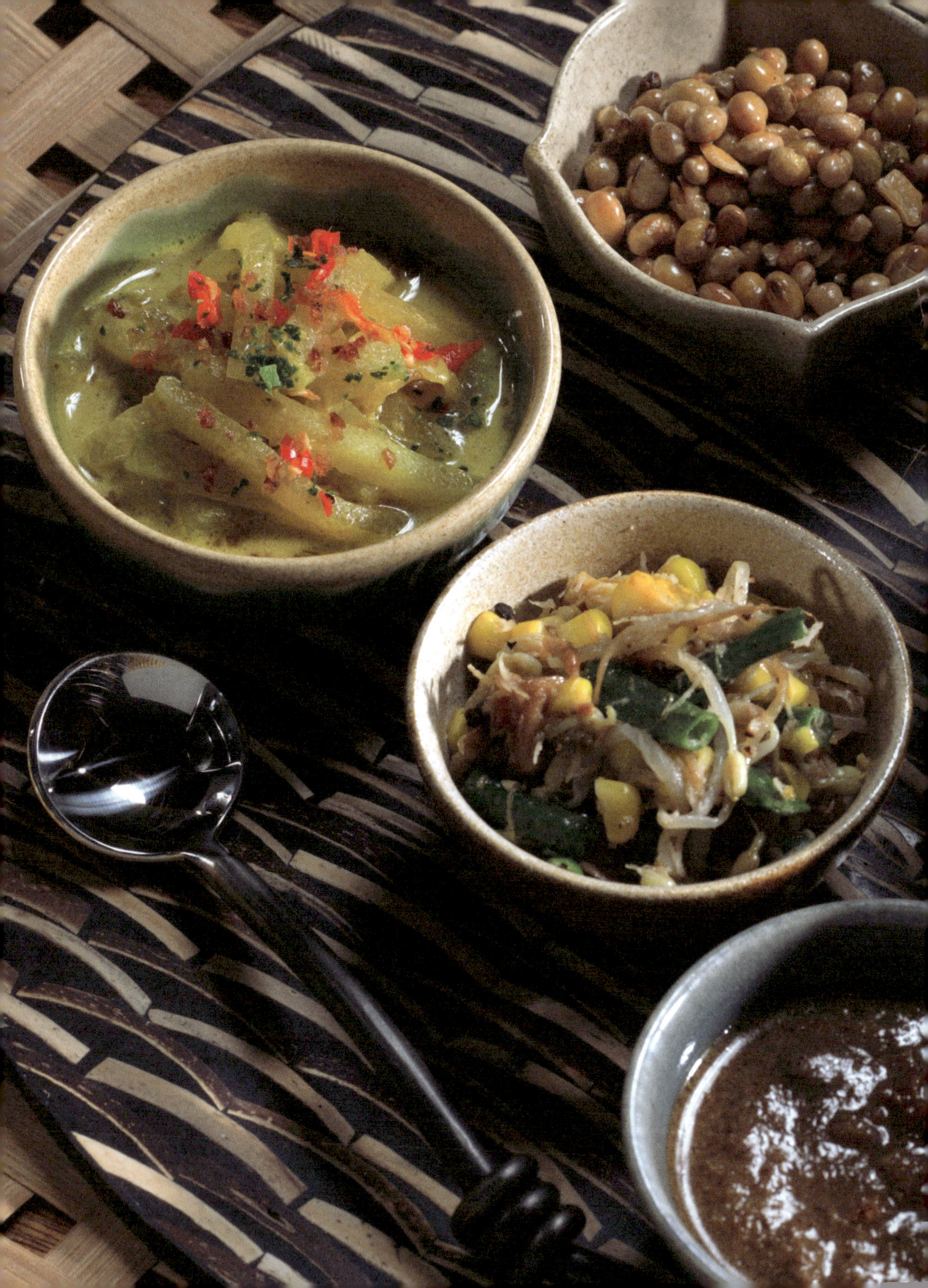

Vegetables & Salads

Pecelan (Vegetable Salad in Peanut Dressing) *68*

Dojang Nuru (Beef Salad with Lime and Mint) *70*

Sambal Tapa (Tuna Salad with Green Mangoes) *73*

Tahu Goreng Tomat (Fried Bean Curd with Tomatoes) *74*

Pecel Terong (Grilled Eggplant
and Soybean Cake in Peanut Sauce) *77*

Telor Dadar (Omelette with Vegetable Salad
in Peanut Dressing) *78*

Sayur Lodeh (Vegetables Stewed in Coconut Cream) *81*

Pecelan (Vegetable Salad in Peanut Dressing) Serves 4

This is the Balinese version of one of Indonesia's most famous dishes, *gado gado*. The biggest difference between the two versions is the use of water here in Bali for the peanut sauce instead of the coconut milk in Java and also the fact that the Balinese version of the peanut sauce is not cooked but simply ground into a creamy sauce using a stone mortar. Any firm vegetable of your choice or simply one vegetable can be used for this very tasty dish.

SALAD

100 g long bean or French beans, cut 3-cm long, blanched

100 g bean sprouts, blanched for 10 seconds in rapidly boiling water

100 g spinach, blanched

100 g small cabbage, thinly sliced and blanched

salt and pepper, to taste

4 hard-boiled quail eggs, peeled and halved

2 tablespoons fried shallots,

2 tablespoons peanuts with skin, fried till golden and crushed

sweet soy sauce *(kecap manis)*, to drizzle

PEANUT SAUCE

1–3 bird's eye chillies, finely sliced

3 garlic cloves, peeled and sliced

25 g lesser galangal *(kencur)* or galangal *(laos)*, finely sliced

250 g peanuts with skin, fried till golden and crushed

20 g palm sugar, chopped

2 tablespoons sweet soy sauce *(kecap manis)*

250 ml water

1 tablespoon tamarind pulp, soaked in 100 ml warm water for 15 minutes and strained

1. Prepare peanut sauce. Combine chillies, garlic and galangal or lesser galangal in a stone mortar or food processor and grind finely. Add peanuts, palm sugar, sweet soy sauce and continue to grind into a fine paste, by gradually adding water and tamarind juice, slowly working the paste into a creamy sauce.

2. Combine vegetables and peanut sauce and blend well. Season to taste with salt and pepper.

3. Garnish with quail egg, fried shallots, peanuts and drizzle sweet soy sauce around.

As mentioned above, there are countless ways of preparing this delicious tasty vegetarian delight. In Bali, cooks often add diced rice cakes to the vegetables and top the salad with a deep-fried duck egg. In Sumatra, I have come across several versions using egg or vermicelli noodles and in Java I enjoyed a popular version that blended diced cooked potatoes with the vegetables.

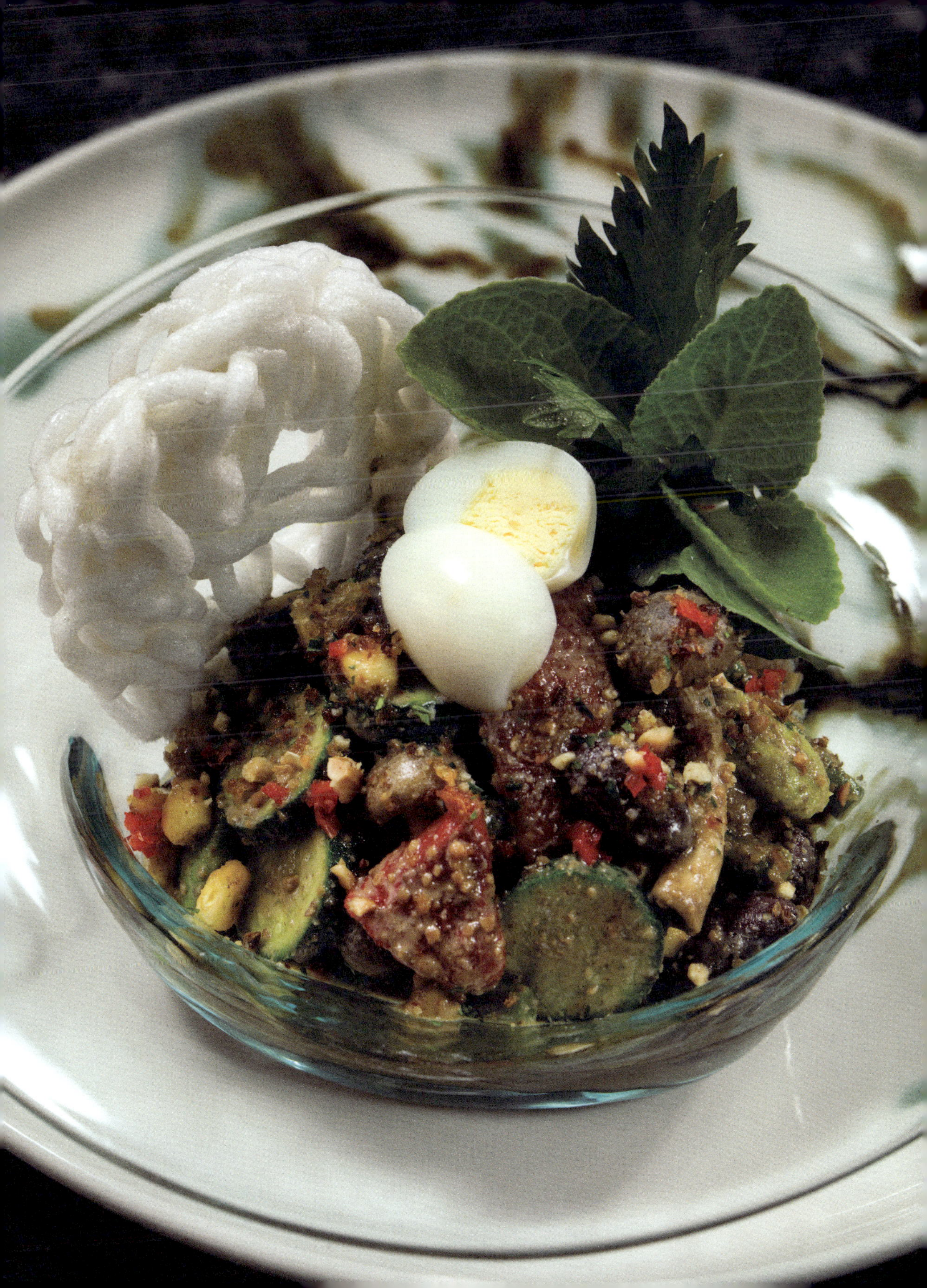

Dojang Nuru (Beef Salad with Lime and Mint)
Serves 4–6

Pork or chicken can be substituted in place of beef in this tasty recipe. The preparation process is the same, regardless of the meat used in the recipe. For pork, use a lean cut. When using chicken, slowly boil a whole chicken in chicken stock or use leftover roasted chicken that has been finely shredded.

60 ml water

3 stalks lemongrass, bruised

5 *salam* leaves

¾ tablespoon salt

60 ml vegetable or coconut oil

800 g beef, top side cut into 4 steaks of 200 g each

1 litre *kuah Indonesia* (page 10)

2 stalks lemongrass, bruised

3 kaffir lime leaves, bruised

salt and ground white pepper, to taste

fresh lime wedges, to garnish

sprigs of fresh mint, to garnish

SPICE BLEND

100 g large red chillies halved, seeded and sliced

3–5 bird's eye chillies, finely sliced

30 g garlic, peeled and sliced

60 g shallots, peeled and sliced

30 g ginger, peeled and sliced

30 g galangal *(laos)*, peeled and sliced

30 g turmeric, peeled and sliced

20 g candlenuts

1 teaspoon crushed black pepper corns

½ teaspoon crushed coriander seeds

½ teaspoon caraway seeds

¼ teaspoon ground nutmeg

20 g palm sugar, chopped

45 ml coconut oil

DRESSING

60 g shallots, peeled and finely sliced

2 large red chillies, halved, seeded and finely sliced

150 g coconut, roughly grated and steamed for 3 minutes and cooled

4 tablespoons roughly chopped lemon basil (*kemangi*)

2 tablespoons roughly chopped fresh mint

4 tablespoons lime juice

salt, to taste

ground white pepper, to taste

1. Prepare spice blend. Combine all ingredients in a stone mortar or food processor and grind into a fine paste. Place ground ingredients into saucepan, then add water, lemongrass, 2 *salam* leaves and salt. Simmer over medium heat for approximately 20 minutes or until water has evaporated and marinade changes to a golden colour. Alternatively pressure cook ingredients for 10 minutes. Cool before using.

2. Heat 60 ml oil in frying pan and quickly sear beef steaks over very high heat until golden on each side. Set steaks aside to cool to room temperature.

3. Coat steaks evenly with spice blend and place into a pressure cooker.

4. Fill pressure cooker with simmering *kuah Indonesia*. Add lemongrass, remaining 3 *salam* and kaffir lime leaves, then bring to a simmer. Remove scum as it accumulates. Pressure cook at 1 bar /15 psi for 45 minutes. Remove pot from heat and allow pot to cool for 30 minutes. Cool beef in *kuah Indonesia* to room temperature.

5. To check if beef is soft, tender and fully cooked, insert a *sate* skewer into centre of meat. Lift meat out of *kuah Indonesia* with skewer. If meat slides off easily and skewer is dry, then meat is done.

6. Cut meat into slivers.

7. Combine meat with all ingredients for the dressing. Mix well.

8. Season to taste with salt and ground white pepper.

9. Garnish as desired.

Alternatively, select a tender cut like sirloin or tenderloin, cut into 150 g steaks. Season steaks evenly on both sides with spice blend and grill or pan-fry to your liking. Allow steaks to cool to room temperature once cooked.

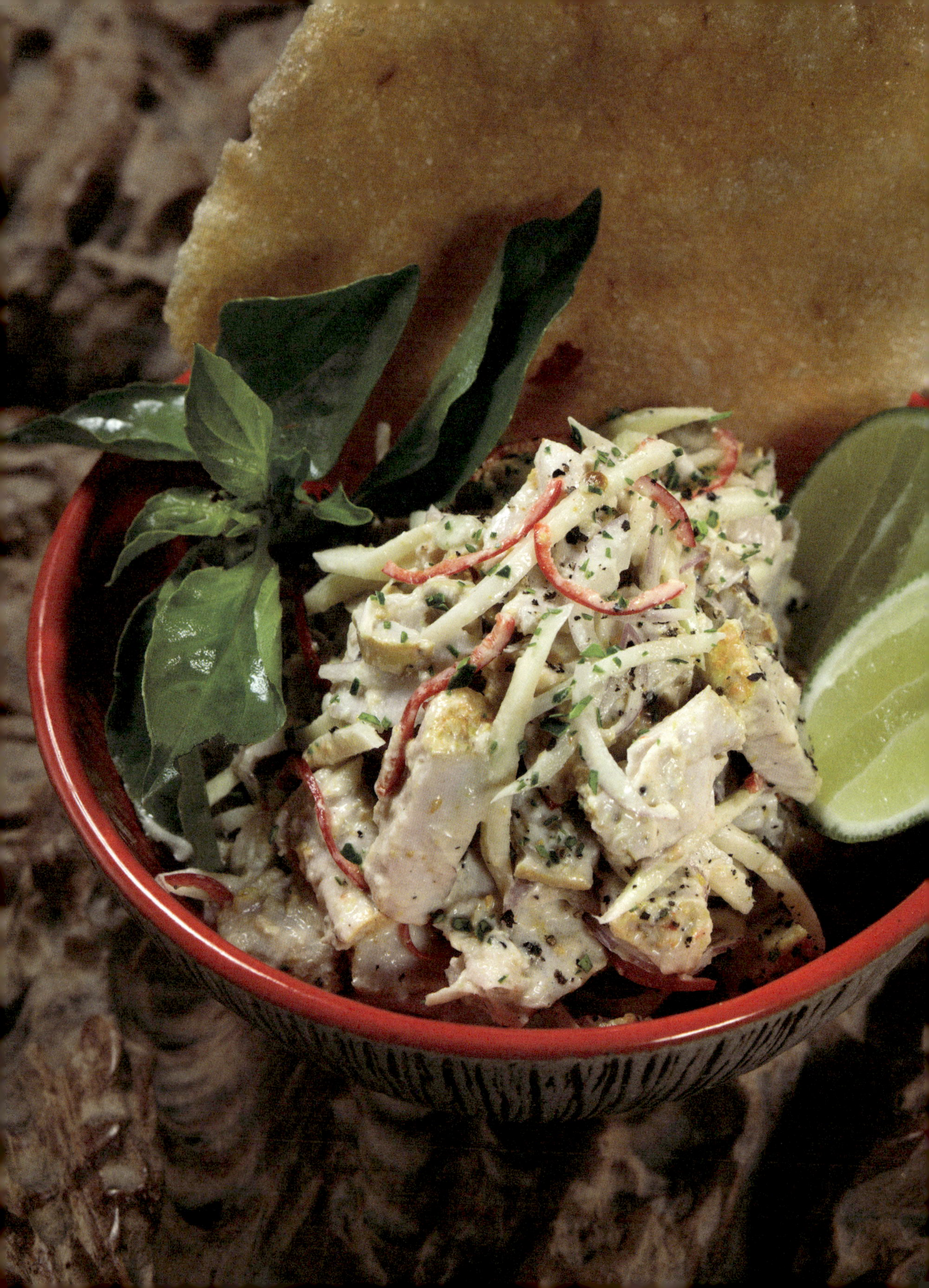

Sambal Tapa (Tuna Salad with Green Mangoes)
Serves 4–6

Tuna can be replaced with mackerels or any other firm white fish. Be careful to keep the temperature as low as possible when cooking tuna as the fish dries out very quickly. Here in Indonesia, this delightful dish is not actually eaten as a salad, but as a main course served with a generous helping of rice. Many cooks in eastern Indonesia love to add a few finely chopped bird's eye chillies as they complement the coconut and lime juice very nicely.

4 tuna steaks, 150 g each
½ teaspoon salt
½ teaspoon crushed black pepper
1 tablespoon lime juice
100 ml coconut or vegetable oil
2 green mangoes, 200 g each, peeled and coarsely shredded
1 tablespoon salt
50 g shallots, peeled and sliced
125 ml coconut cream
salt and pepper, to taste

1. Season tuna steaks with salt, black pepper and lime juice. Keep tuna refrigerated to prevent steaks from cooking when searing.

2. Heat coconut or vegetable oil in frying pan until very hot. Sear each tuna steak quickly until golden on both sides. This should take less then 20 seconds for one steak. You do not want to cook the steaks. Searing will add a lot of flavour to the dish. Cool steaks to room temperature and allow oil to drip off.

3. Place two steaks into a foodsafe heatproof plastic bag and seal.

4. Vacuum cook at 50°C for 20 minutes. Place bags into iced water and chill.

5. Remove tuna steaks from bags and finely flake tuna.

6. Combine mangoes with salt. Mix well and set aside for 10 minutes.

7. Squeeze to remove sour liquid.

8. Combine all ingredients, mix well and season to taste with salt and pepper.

9. Garnish as desired. Serve with lime wedges.

Alternatively, you can also pan-fry steaks over very low heat until medium rare or insert a meat thermometer into the centre of the steaks and cook, after searing them at a temperature of 50°C in the centre in a oven that is set at 80°C.

Tahu Goreng Tomat (Fried Bean Curd with Tomatoes)
Serves 4–6

Tofu and *tempeh* are relatively recent introductions into the diet of many people living in the rural areas in Indonesia, but they already feature in many delicious dishes such as this one.

8 firm pieces of bean curd, approximately 25 g each

2 tablespoons *bumbu sayur* (page 9)

1 pinch salt

2 tablespoons rice flour

oil for frying

sprigs of lemon basil (*kemangi*) and spring onions (scallions), to garnish

DRESSING

4 tablespoons coconut or vegetable oil

60 g shallots, peeled and sliced

200 g tomatoes, peeled, halved, seeded and diced or sliced or cherry tomatoes, peeled

1 tablespoon palm sugar

5–7 bird's eye chillies, finely sliced

1 tablespoon tamarind pulp, soaked in 50 ml warm water for 15 minutes and strained

2 tablespoons lime juice

4 tablespoons lemon basil (*kemangi*), roughly chopped

salt, to taste

crushed white peppercorns, to taste

1. Marinate bean curd with 2 tablespoons *bumbu sayur* and a pinch of salt. Mix well. Dust evenly with rice flour, and deep-fry in medium-hot oil (150°C) until golden and crispy. Set aside to drain.

2. Prepare dressing. Heat oil in a saucepan. Add shallots and sauté until fragrant. Remove from heat and cool.

3. Add remaining ingredients and mix well. Toss bean curd with dressing and garnish with sprigs of lemon basil and spring onions.

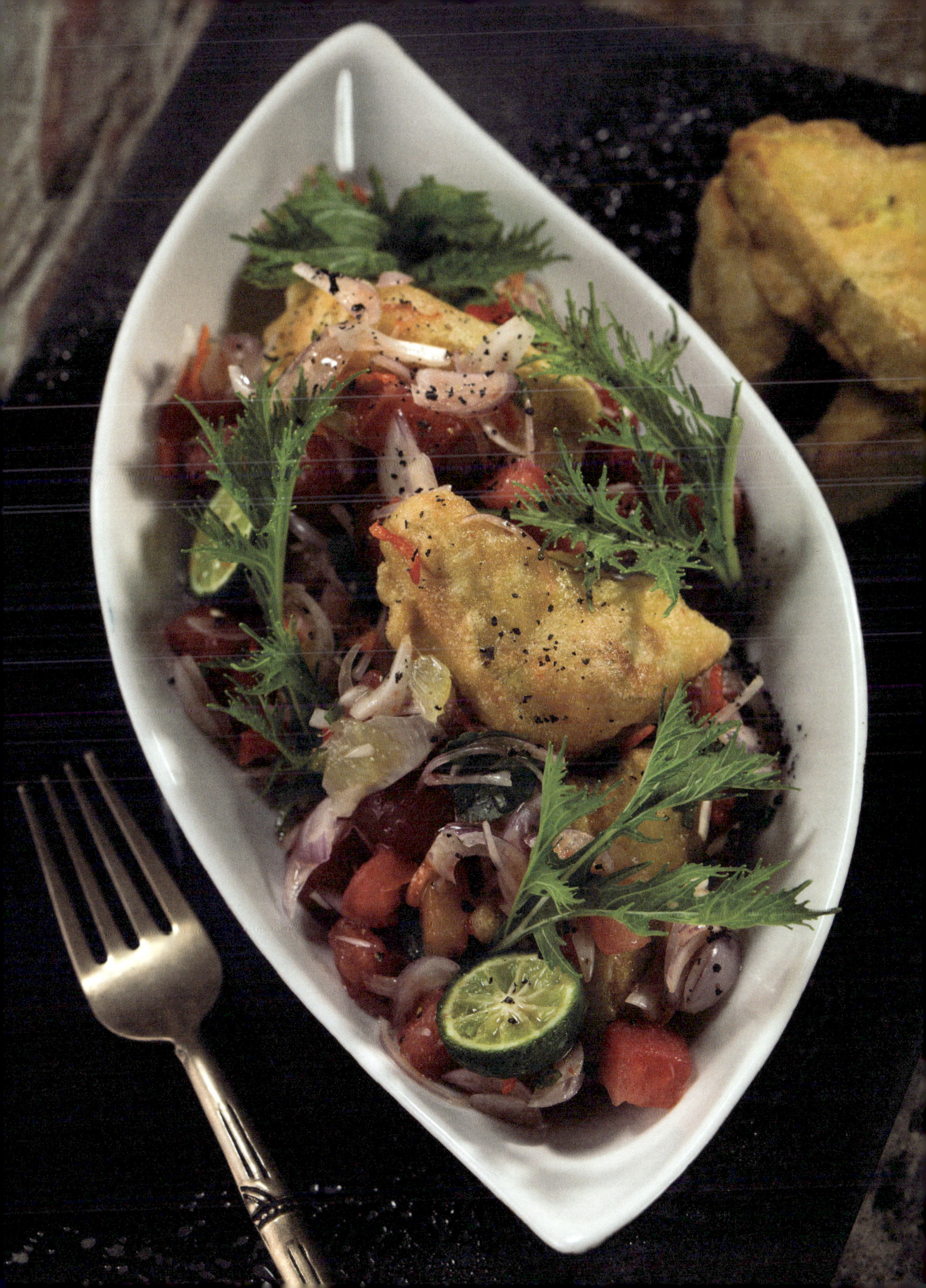

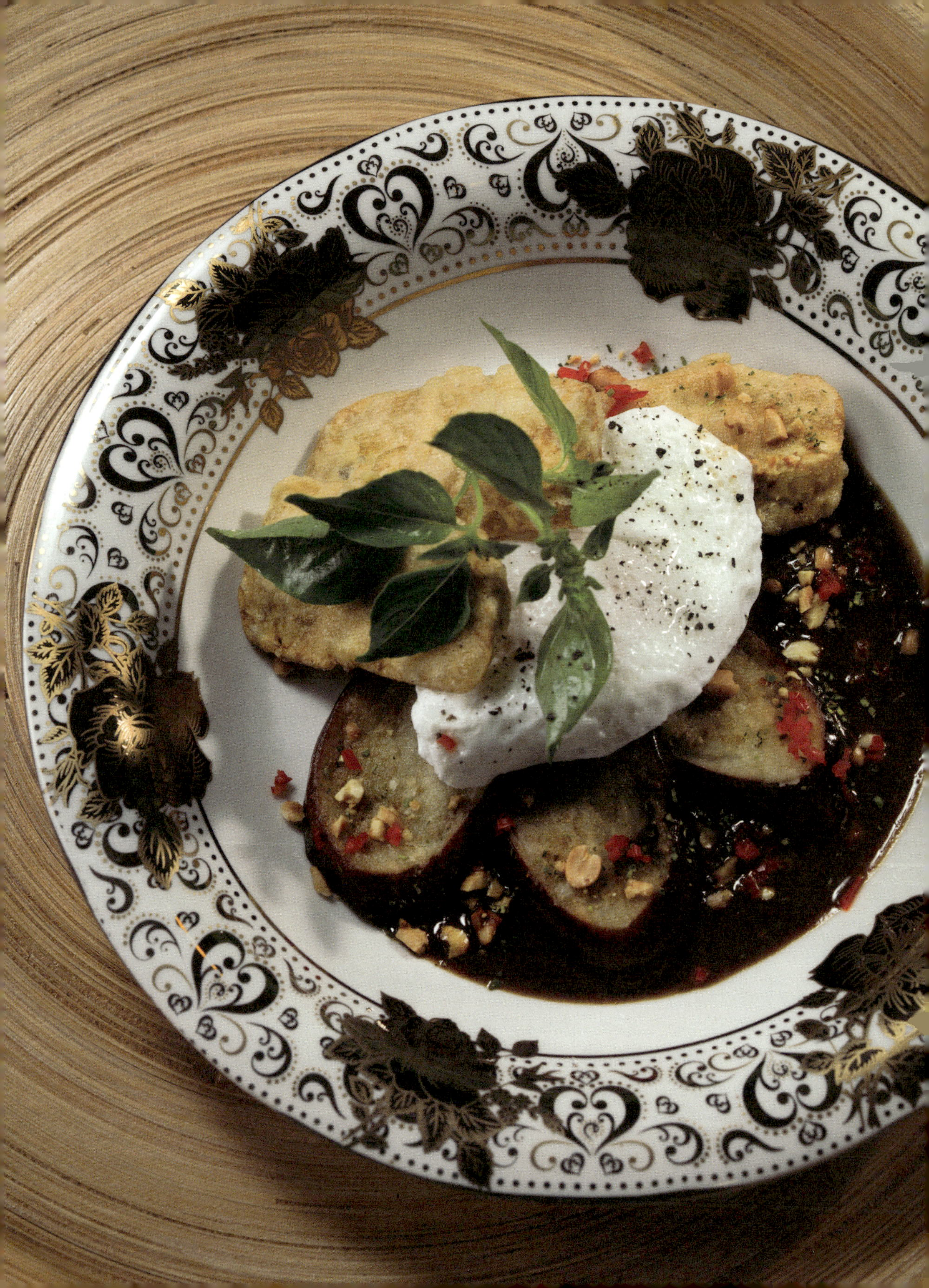

Pecel Terong (Grilled Eggplant and Soybean Cake in Peanut Sauce) Serves 4

It is difficult to estimate how much water to add when preparing the peanut sauce. It is best to have perhaps half a litre of warm water next to the stone mortar. Then while grinding the peanuts into a smooth paste, gradually add more water until the sauce is smooth and creamy.

salt, to taste

lime juice and lime zest, to taste

4 tablespoons coconut or vegetable oil

1 tablespoon coarse salt

400 g eggplants, halved

200 g fermented soybean cake (*tempeh*), sliced and fried till crispy

4 eggs, poached or soft-boiled for 4 minutes and peeled

lemon basil (*kemangi*) for garnish

PEANUT SAUCE

3 tablespoons coconut or vegetable oil

80 g large red chillies, halved, seeded and sliced

3–5 bird's eye chillies, sliced

20 g garlic, peeled and sliced

30 g shallots, peeled and sliced

10 g ginger, peeled and sliced

30 g candlenuts, crushed

1 tablespoon grated palm sugar

5 kaffir lime leaves, bruised

250 g raw peanuts with skins, deep-fried or roasted golden

60 ml coconut cream

1 tablespoon tamarind pulp, soaked in 100 ml warm water for 15 minutes and strained

water, as required

1. Prepare peanut sauce. Heat oil in a heavy saucepan. Add all ingredients except peanuts, coconut cream, tamarind juice and water, and sauté over medium heat for 5 minutes or until fragrant. Set aside to cool.

2. Place fried ingredients into a stone mortar or food processor and grind into a fine paste. Add peanuts and continue to grind into a creamy sauce, gradually adding coconut cream, tamarind juice and water.

3. Place peanut sauce into saucepan and bring to a boil. Reduce heat and simmer until sauce slightly thickens. Add more water if sauce is too thick. Sauce should be served creamy and warm. Season to taste with salt, lime juice and lime zest.

4. Combine oil with salt and blend well. Brush eggplants with salt-oil blend and marinate for 10 minutes.

5. Grill over medium hot charcoal until eggplants are soft and skin comes easily off.

6. Pour a generous amount of sauce on centre of plate and top with fried soybean cake, eggplants and poached or soft-boiled eggs. Garnish with lemon basil.

Telor Dadar (Omelette with Vegetable Salad in Peanut Dressing) Serves 4

Here we have a reflection of the availability of produces in a every day market. This recipe was taken from my mother-in-law's kitchen and has frequently ended up on our dining table. What I really enjoy is the combination of a soft moist vegetable omelette that is topped with warm vegetable salad in a creamy peanut dressing.

OMELETTE

3 tablespoons coconut or vegetable oil

40 g shallots, peeled and sliced

30 g garlic, peeled and sliced

3–5 bird's eye chillies, finely sliced

80 g celery, peeled and sliced

80 g leek, finely sliced

80 g spring onions (scallions), finely sliced

80 g tomatoes, halved, seeded and diced

12 eggs, beaten

SALAD

100 g bean sprouts, blanched for 1 minute

100 g green beans, finely sliced and blanched for 1 minute

100 g tomatoes, halved, seeded and diced

salt, to taste

lime juice, to taste

PEANUT DRESSING

100 g raw peanuts with skin, deep-fried or roasted golden brown

2 bird's eye chillies, finely sliced

2 garlic cloves, peeled and sliced

10 g ginger, peeled and sliced

½ teaspoon palm sugar, chopped

1 tablespoon sweet soy sauce *(kecap manis)*

100 ml water

1 pinch salt

1 tablespoon fresh lime juice + more to taste

1. Prepare omelette. Heat oil in a non-stick pan, add shallots, garlic and chillies and sauté until fragrant and lightly golden.

2. Add celery, leek and spring onions and continue to sauté for 2 more minutes over moderate heat. Add tomatoes and mix well.

3. Add eggs and cook until fluffy, constantly moving pan and stirring with a spatula.

4. Reduce stirring and tilt pan gently to slide omelette to front. Roll one end of omelette forward and fold to give omelette an oval shape.

5. Prepare peanut dressing. Combine all ingredients in a stone mortar or food processor and grind into smooth sauce, adding more water if required to achieve desired consistency. Season to taste with a pinch of salt and more lime juice.

6. Prepare salad. Combine peanut dressing with bean sprouts, green beans and tomatoes and blend well.

7. Season to taste with salt and lime juice.

8. Top omelette with salad and serve with vegetable crackers.

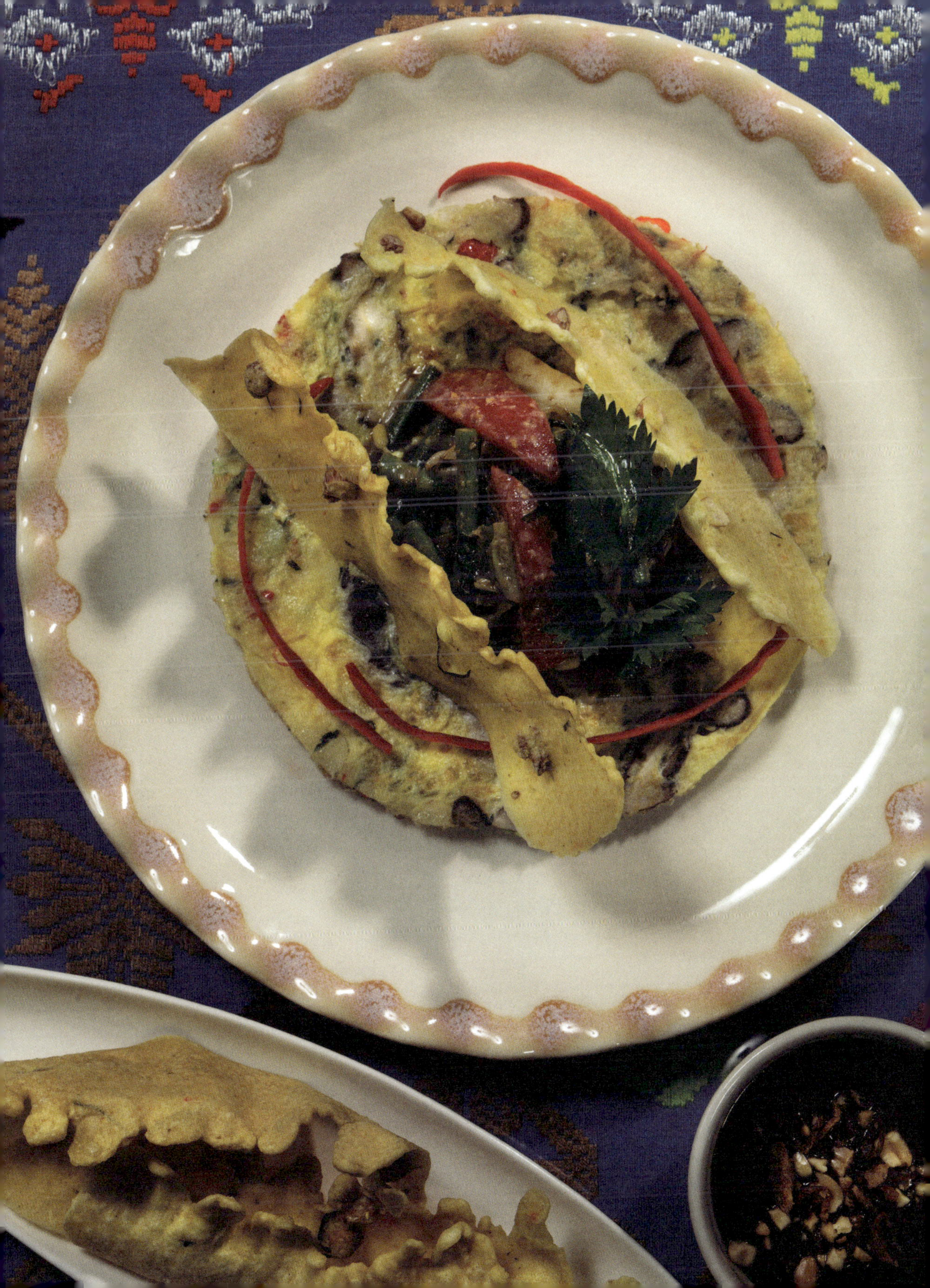

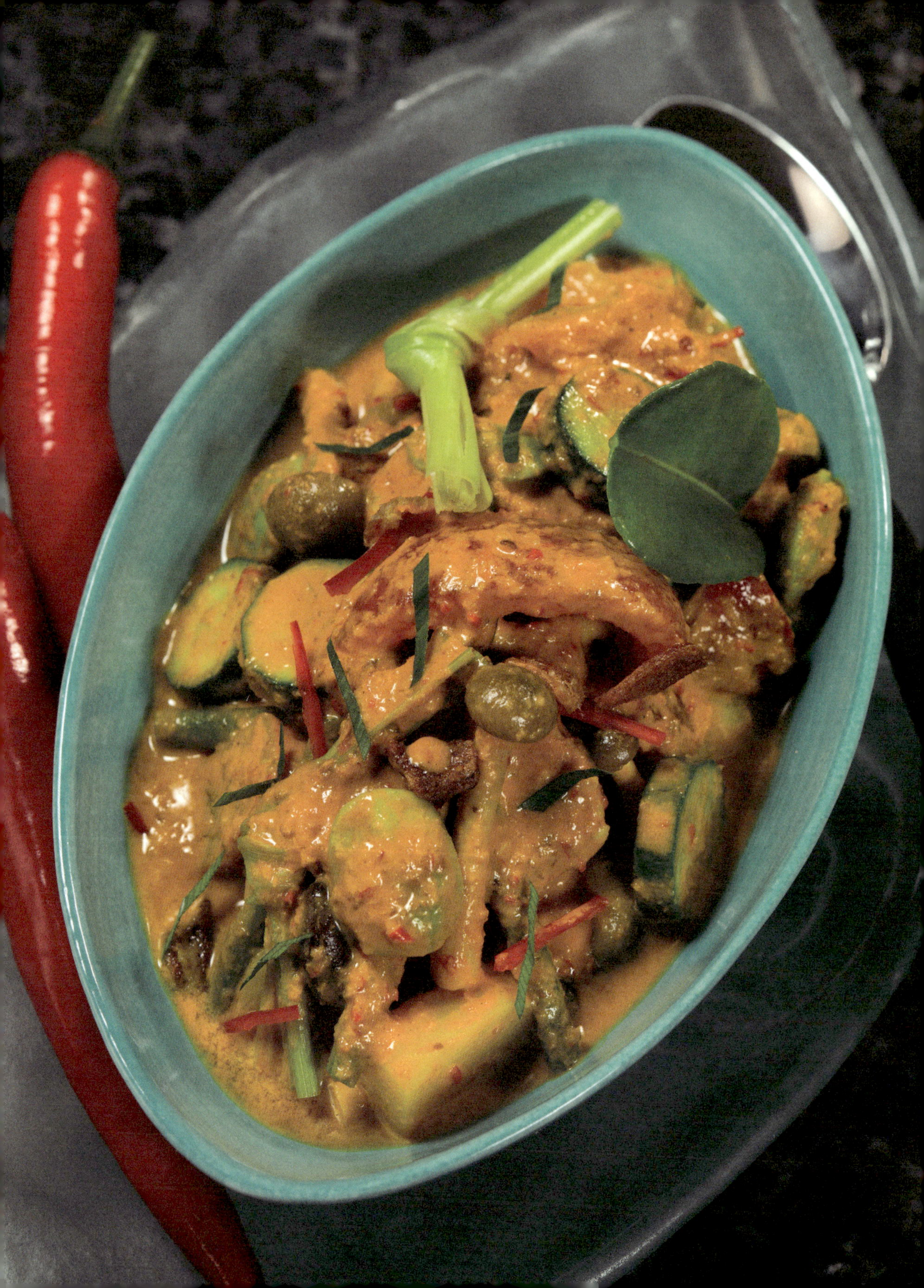

Sayur Lodeh (Vegetables Stewed in Coconut Cream) Serves 4

This dish makes use of local vegetables, coconut cream and spices that are available throughout the country, and different cooks prepare this dish differently. This delicious vegetable dish tastes terrific with any grilled fish or meat.

- 75 g green papayas, peeled, seeded and cut in ¾-cm cubes
- 2 tablespoons coconut or vegetable oil
- 2 stalks lemongrass, bruised
- 3 *salam* leaves
- 2 kaffir lime leaves, bruised
- 375 ml *kaldu sayur* or *kuah Indonesia* (page 11 or 10)
- 125 ml coconut cream
- 50 g bean sprouts, blanched for 30 seconds
- 50 g corn kernels, blanched
- 50 g white cabbage, cut into 3 x 1-cm cubes and blanched
- 50 g Melinjo leaves cleaned (if not available substitute with spinach)
- 100 g baby eggplants, cut into quarters
- 50 g shiitake mushrooms, sliced or whole (Any mushroom works as well)
- 100 g fermented soybean cake *(tempeh)*, diced into 2 x 1-cm cubes, dusted with rice flour and deep-fried till golden
- 80 g tomatoes or cherry tomatoes, peeled (large tomatoes seeded and sliced, cherry tomatoes only halved)
- salt and black pepper, to taste

SPICE PASTE

- 40 g shallots, peeled and sliced
- 30 g garlic, peeled and sliced
- 50 g large red chillies, halved, seeded and sliced
- 20 g ginger, peeled and sliced
- 20 g galangal *(laos)*, peeled and sliced
- 20 g turmeric, peeled and sliced
- ½ teaspoon salt
- 1 teaspoon roasted dried shrimp paste *(terasi)*

1. Simmer papaya cubes in water for several minutes until almost soft, then drain water. Set aside.

2. Prepare spice paste. Combine shallots, garlic, chillies, ginger, galangal, turmeric, salt and shrimp paste in a stone mortar or food processor and grind into a fine paste.

3. Heat oil in saucepan, add ground spices, lemongrass, *salam* and kaffir lime leaves and sauté until fragrant.

4. Fill saucepan with *kaldu sayur* or *kuah Indonesia* and bring to a simmer.

5. Add coconut cream and bring back to simmer.

6. Add vegetables (except tomatoes) and soybean cakes. Simmer for 5 minutes until sauce becomes lightly creamy.

7. Add tomatoes and bring stew back to a simmer. Season to taste with salt and black pepper.

8. Garnish as desired.

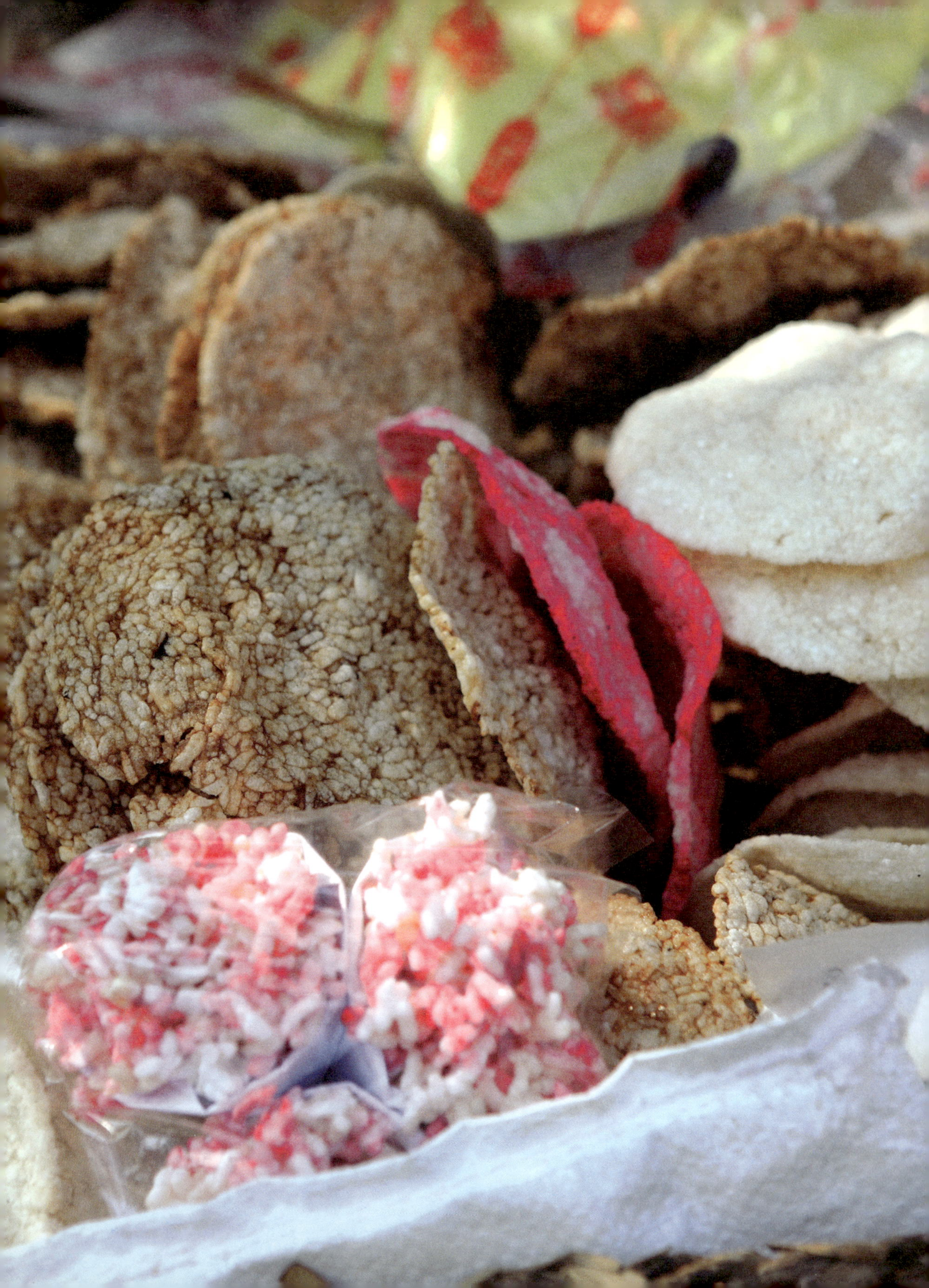

Light Meals & Snacks

Rujak (Fruit Salad in Tamarind Chilli Sauce) 85

Pisang Goreng dan Sambal Tomat Pedas
(Fried Bananas with Sweet Chilli Sauce) 86

Bubuh Injin (Black Rice Pudding) 89

Bergedel Jagung (Sweet Corn Pancakes) 90

Tempeh Manis Kacang
(Crispy Fried Soybean Cakes with Peanuts) 93

Es Cendol (Iced Fruits in Coconut Dressing) 94

Dadar (Coconut Pancake) 97

Jaja Sumping Nangka (Steamed Jackfruit Cake) 98

Sumping Waluh (Steamed Pumpkin Cake) 101

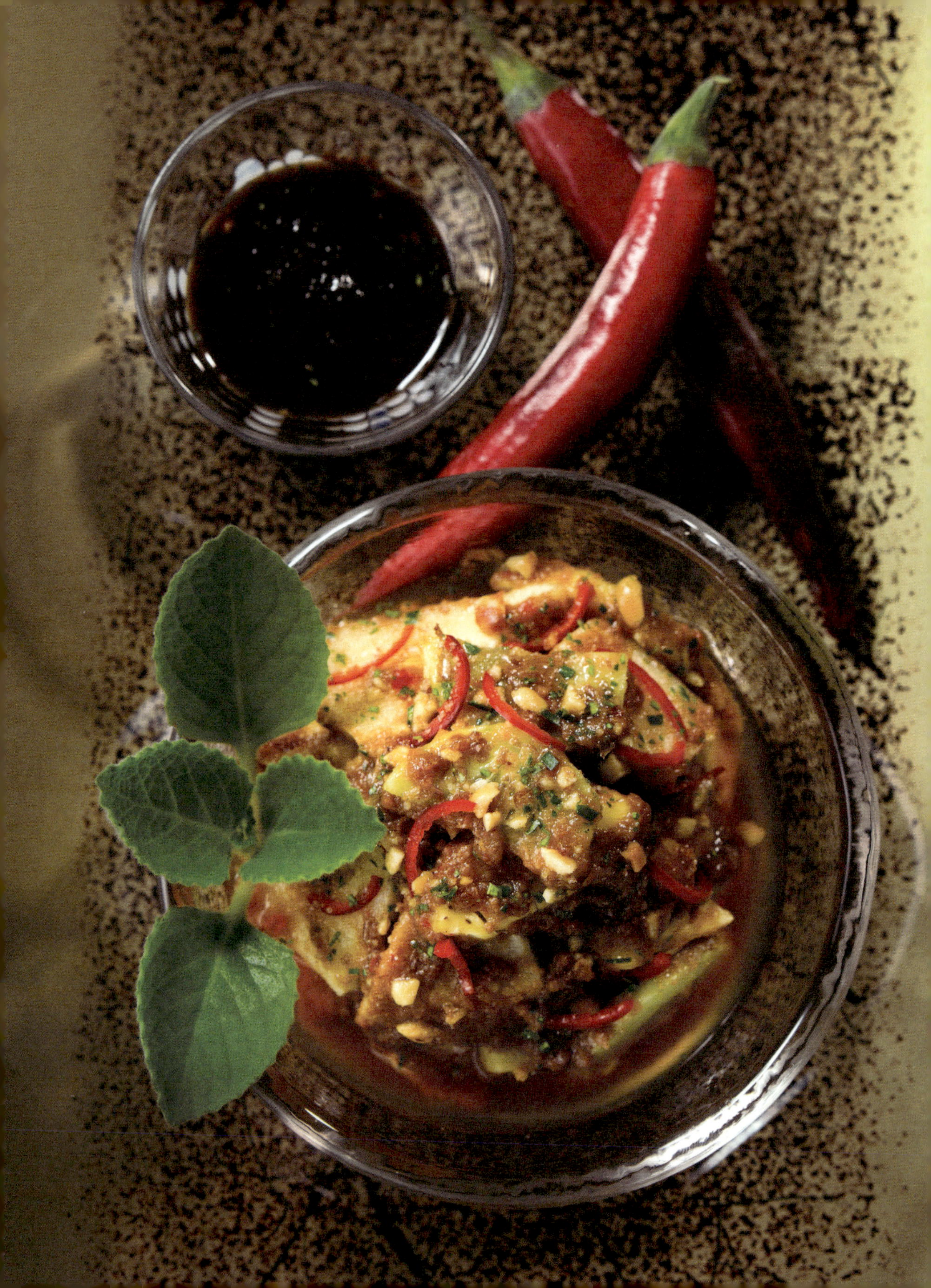

Rujak (Fruit Salad in Tamarind Chilli Sauce) Serves 4

One of the most popular snacks in Bali, and indeed in all of Indonesia, *rujak* is a mixture of crispy, sliced fruits served with sweet and sour sauce. It is best to use crispy fruits to give the dish its desired texture. Although these snacks are easily available from push carts throughout Indonesia, the locals like to make them from fruits grown in their own backyards.

75 g pineapple, peeled and sliced

75 g green mango, peeled and sliced

75 g green papaya, peeled, seeded and sliced

75 g cucumber, peeled, halved, seeded and sliced

75 g water apple, cut into quarters

75 g Hikkoman yam bean, peeled and sliced

SAUCE

250 ml palm sugar syrup

1 teaspoon roasted and crumbled dried shrimp paste (*terasi*)

4–6 bird's eye chillies, finely sliced

100 g tamarind pulp, soaked in 120 ml warm water for 15 minutes and strained

salt, to taste

1. Prepare sauce. Place palm sugar syrup, shrimp paste and chillies in a stone mortar or food processor and grind to a very fine paste. Gradually add tamarind juice and blend until smooth. Season to taste with salt.

2. Combine all fruits and vegetables in a deep bowl. Add sauce and toss well.

Pisang Goreng dan Sambal Tomat Pedas
(Fried Bananas with Sweet Chilli Sauce) Serves 4–6

We discovered this unusual combination of fried bananas and sweet chilli sauce in a seaside restaurant on the island of Ternate. The people of Ternate call the sauce *pedas*, which means hot and spicy but this is an overstatement as the sugar and lime juice balances the spiciness perfectly.

FRIED BANANAS

100 g plain flour
250 ml water
1 pinch salt
8 finger bananas or large bananas
45 g rice flour
oil for frying

SWEET CHILLI SAUCE

150 g large red chillies
25 g bird's eye chillies
50 g shallots, peeled and halved
200 g tomatoes, peeled and seeded
¼ teaspoon roasted dried shrimp paste *(terasi)*
25 g palm sugar, chopped
25 g sugar
50 ml coconut oil
2 tablespoons lime juice
salt, to taste

1. Prepare fried bananas. Combine plain flour, water and salt in a deep mixing bowl. Whisk vigorously until batter is even, smooth and not too thin, and has the consistency of a pancake mix.

2. Dust bananas evenly with rice flour. Dip bananas into batter until well coated.

3. Heat a generous amount of oil in a heavy saucepan to about 120°C.

4. Add bananas and simultaneously increase temperature of oil slowly to around 160°C, which should take about 20 minutes. Remove and drain for 1 minute on kitchen towels.

5. Prepare sweet chilli sauce. Grill red chillies, bird's eye chillies, shallots and tomatoes until skins are evenly black. Peel skins and remove all seeds from large chillies and tomatoes.

6. Place chillies, shallots, tomatoes, shrimp paste, palm sugar, sugar and coconut oil into a stone mortar or food processor and grind into a coarse, creamy paste.

7. Season to taste with lime juice and salt.

8. Serve fried bananas with sweet chilli sauce on the side.

Sweet potatoes and jackfruit can be fried in the same way.

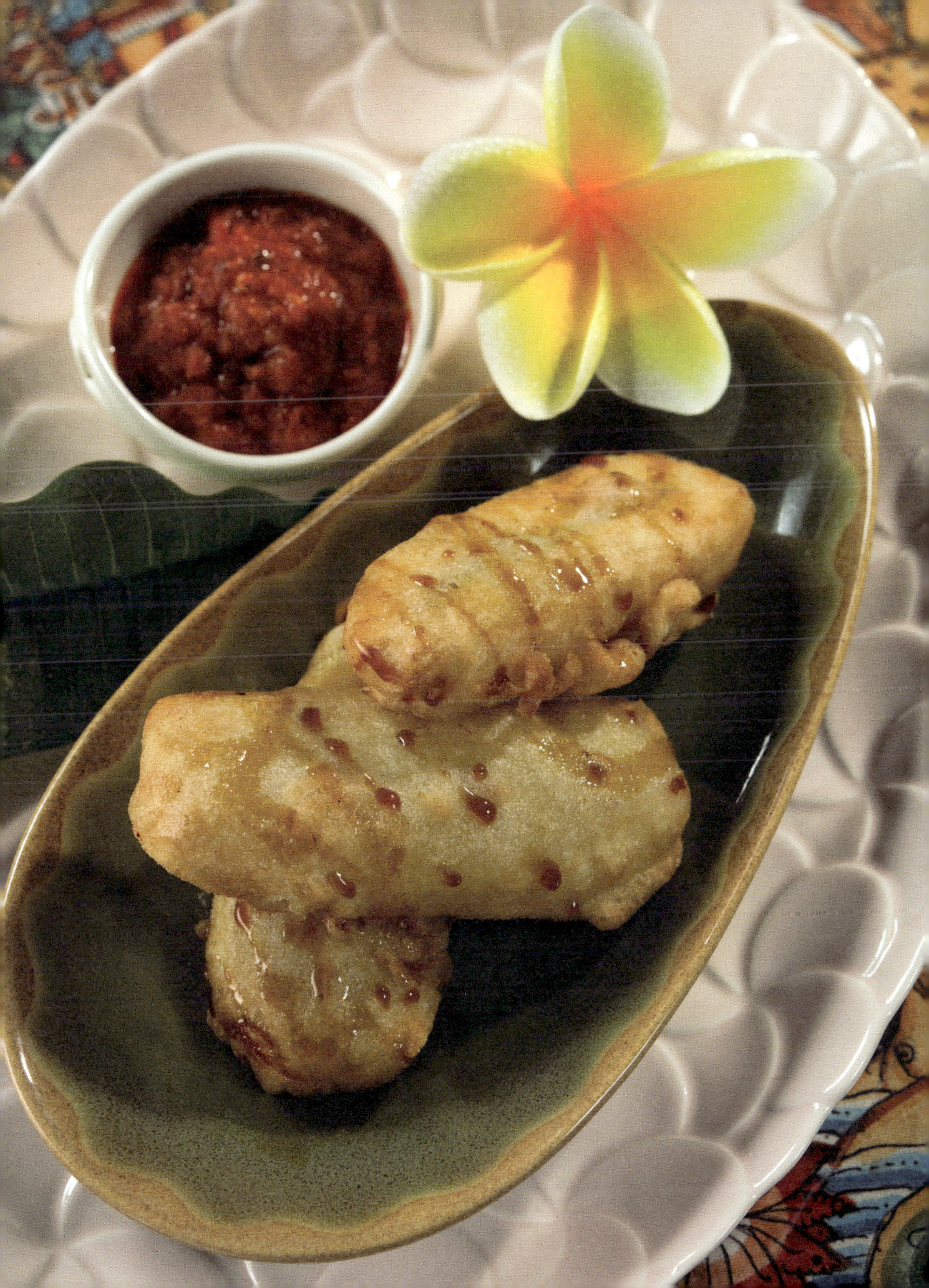

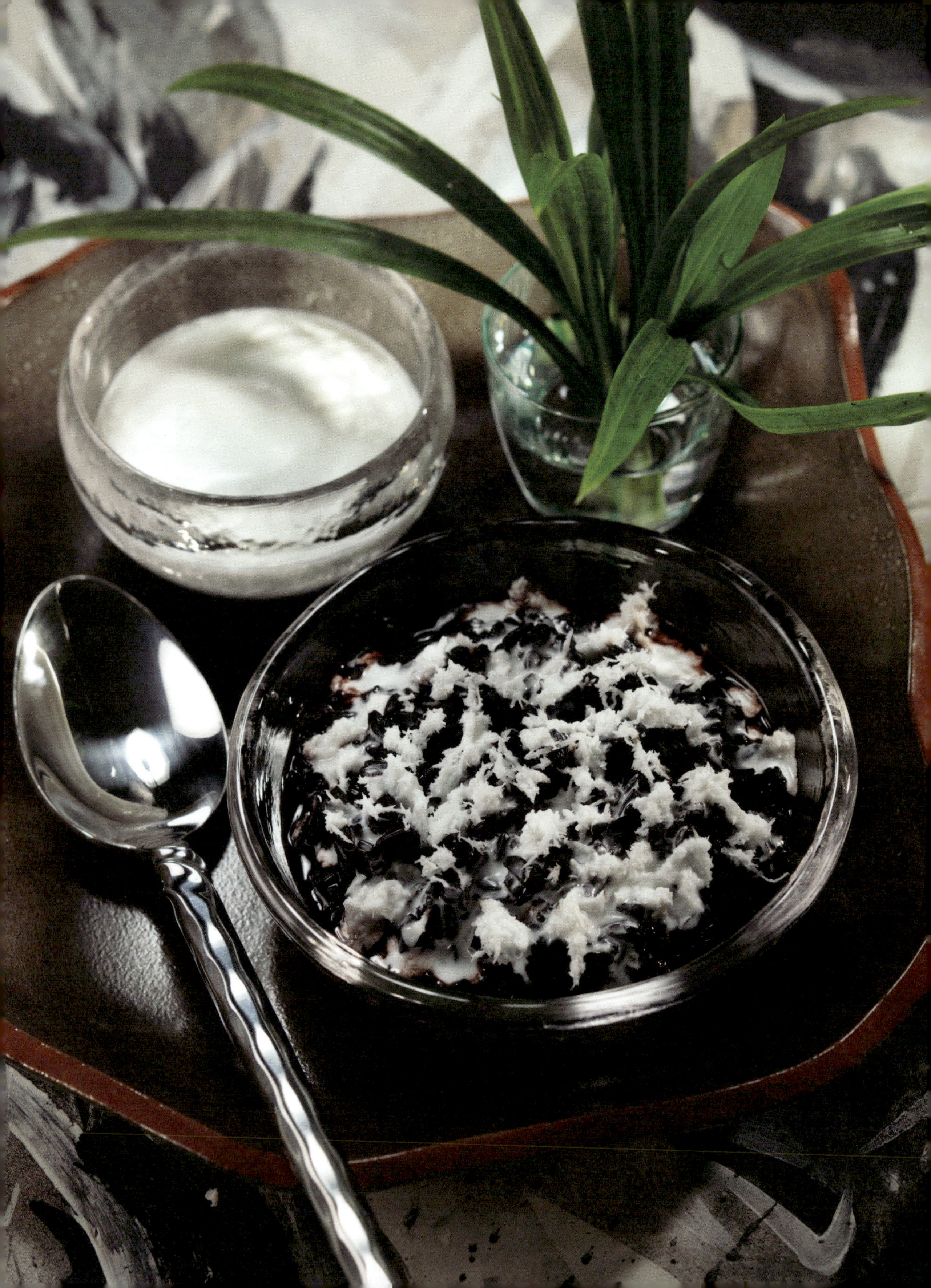

Bubuh Injin (Black Rice Pudding) Serves 4–6

Bubuh injin translates into "black rice porridge", which is actually misleading as the final dish must have the consistency of a risotto. The dish should look very black and be like a porridge, but the rice grains must still be slightly "al dente". If pandan is difficult to find, replace with cinnamon or even a vanilla bean.

250 g black glutinous rice
50 g white glutinous rice
800 ml water or a very light coconut milk
2 pandan leaves, torn
100–125 g palm sugar, chopped to taste
1 pinch salt
125 ml coconut cream

1. Rinse both black and white glutinous rice well for 2 minutes under running water. Drain. Soak in water or coconut milk for 8 hours. Drain.

2. Place water, both black and white glutinous rice and pandan leaves in a saucepan and simmer over very low heat for 45 minutes. Stir frequently stirring prevent rice from sticking to pan.

3. Alternatively, place water, both black and white glutinous rice and pandan leaves into a pressure cooker. Quickly bring to a boil.

4. Pressure cook at 1 bar / 15 psi for 15 minutes. Turn off heat and allow to cool for 30 minutes before opening pressure cooker.

5. Add palm sugar and continue to simmer until a smooth, slightly runny consistency similar to a risotto is achieved. Season with a pinch of salt. Remove from heat and allow to cool to room temperature

6. When serving, top with a generous amount of coconut cream.

As fresh coconut milk turns rancid fairly quickly, a pinch of salt is usually added to the milk to help preserve it for a few hours. A more effective alternative is to cook the coconut milk with 1 teaspoon cornflour diluted in a little water; heat gently and stir constantly for a couple of minutes. This coconut sauce will keep overnight. Milk made from instant powdered coconut will not turn rancid, although the flavour will not be as good as fresh coconut milk.

Bergedel Jagung (Sweet Corn Pancakes) Serves 4–6

These simple and very delicious pancakes are found throughout Indonesia and yet every cook has his or her own version. Use the following recipe as a guideline and get creative with the dish by adding prawns, crabmeat and diced mushrooms or replace half the corn with soft-boiled and roughly mashed potatoes.

600 g corn kernels
2 tablespoons *bumbu sayur* (page 9)
2 tablespoons plain flour
1 egg
2 tablespoons roughly chopped celery leaves
salt, to taste
1 pinch crushed white peppercorns
oil for frying

1. Place corn kernels into a stone mortar and grind coarsely.

2. Add *bumbu sayur*, flour, egg, celery leaves, salt and peppercorns and continue to grind into a smooth paste.

3. Using a tablespoon, form paste into patties and lower them into medium hot oil. Deep-fry until golden. Alternatively, pan-fry cakes in a non-stick pan with very little oil. Place on kitchen towels to drain excess oil before serving.

Always buy corn with the husk still intact, as the sugar in the kernels transforms into starch the moment the husk is removed.

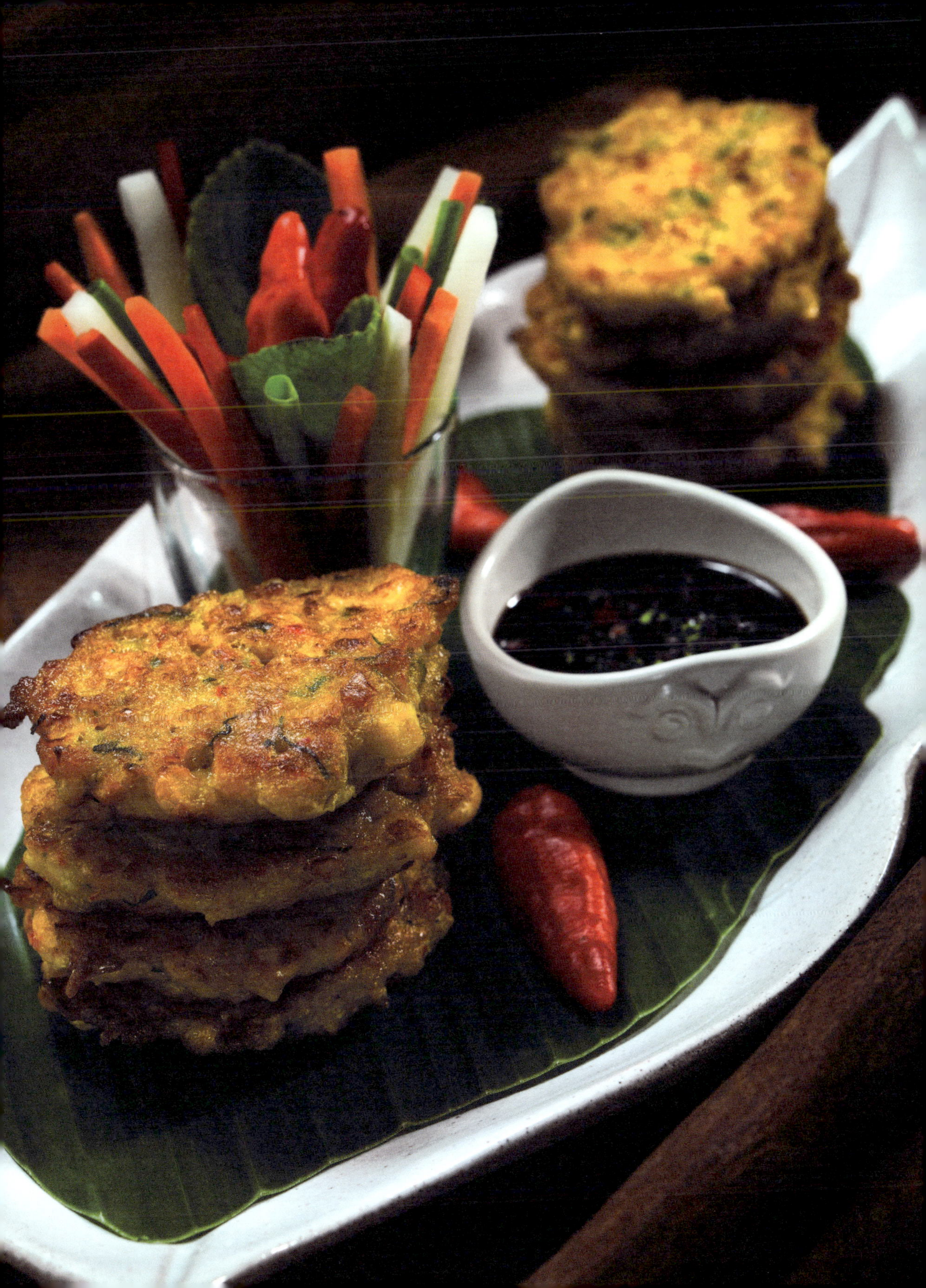

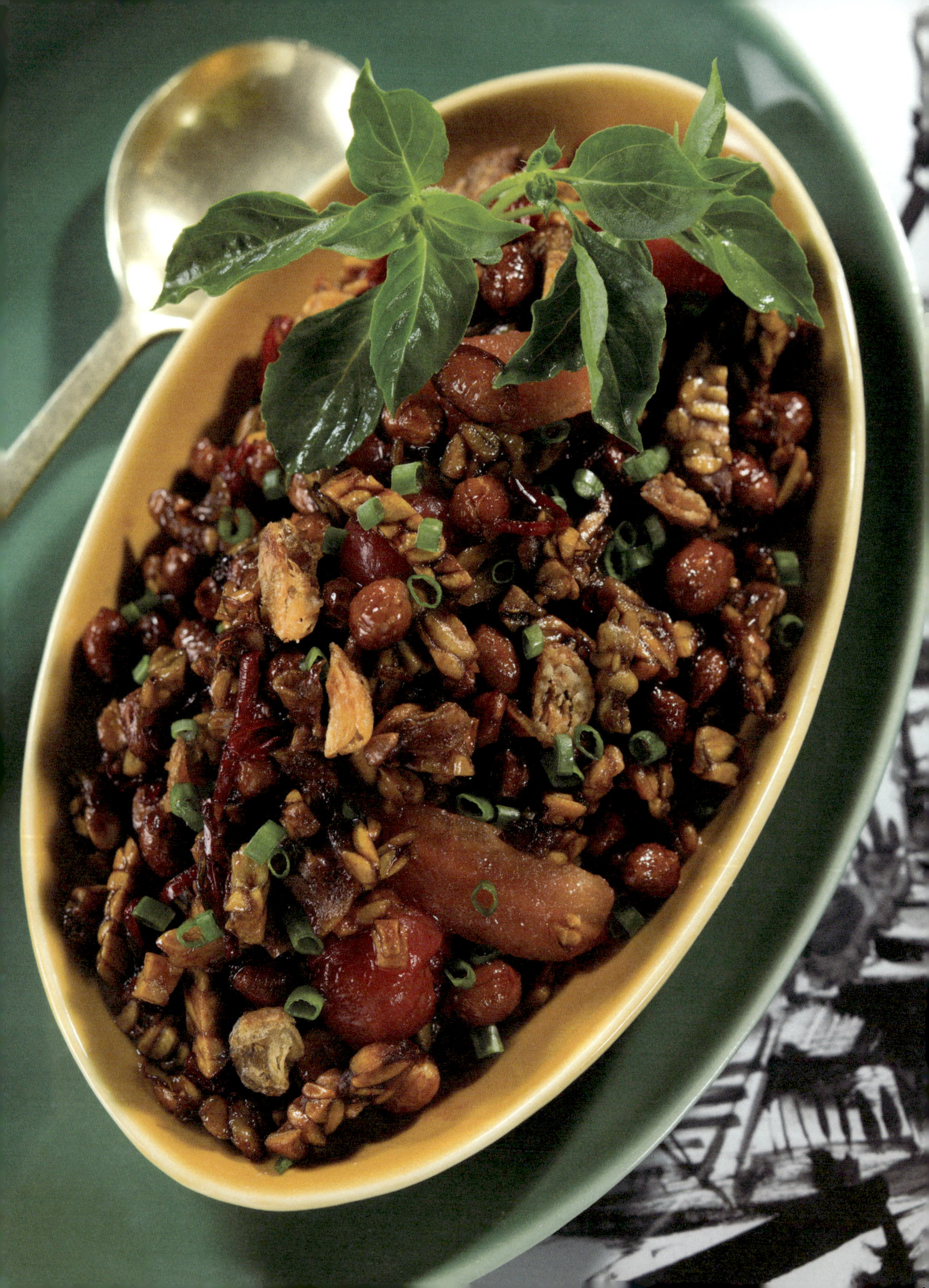

Tempeh Manis Kacang (Crispy Fried Soybean Cakes with Peanuts) Makes 14–15 parcels

Delicious is almost an understatement. Tasty, crunchy, sweet and so simple, this delightful condiment is an everyday favourite. Similar preparations of this dish are found throughout the Indonesian archipelago, but what sets this version apart from any other recipe is the addition of peanuts, which adds a delightful crunchy texture to the classic favourite.

vegetable oil for frying

200 g fermented soybean cake (*tempeh*), sliced into evenly sized strips slightly larger than a matchstick

4 tablespoons coconut or vegetable oil

60 g shallots, peeled and sliced

20 g garlic, peeled and sliced

2 large red chillies, halved, seeded and finely sliced

45 ml sweet soy sauce (*kecap manis*)

60 ml *kaldu sayur* (page 11)

200 g peanuts with skins on, deep-fried or roasted until golden

salt, to taste

ground white pepper, to taste

1. Heat sufficient oil to 150°C for deep-frying. Add sliced soybean cakes and fry till golden. Drain on kitchen towels.

2. Heat 4 tablespoons of vegetable oil in a frying pan. Add shallots, garlic and chillies and sauté over medium heat for 2–4 minutes until translucent and fragrant.

3. Add sweet soy sauce and continue to sauté until evenly glazed.

4. Add *kaldu sayur* and simmer.

5. Add fried soybean cakes and peanuts. Stir-fry until evenly glazed and caramelized.

6. Season to taste with salt and pepper.

Es Cendol (Iced Fruits in Coconut Dressing) Serves 4–6

Cendol is an everyday Indonesian drink. Small pieces of dough are doused in coconut milk, to which sugar is added and then served over plenty of shaved ice. The dough can be made from wheat, tapioca or glutinous rice flour. It is then rolled and shaped into dumplings and boiled in either lightly salted water or palm sugar syrup. To make *cendol*, mix the dumplings with coconut milk, palm sugar syrup, and add ice if available.

SAUCE

350 g palm sugar, chopped

500 ml water

1 pandan leaf, bruised

200 g sweet potatoes, peeled and diced

200 g palm fruits

200 g diced fruits (pineapples, mango, jackfruit and bananas etc.)

50 ml coconut cream

RICE FLOUR DUMPLINGS

150 g glutinous rice flour

50 g tapioca flour

1 pinch salt

160 ml water (depending on the flour and water quality, you might have to add a little more or a little less water. Add half of the given amount of water first and then add the rest tablespoon by tablespoon)

2 tablespoons lime juice

1. Prepare sauce. Bring palm sugar, water and pandan leaf to a boil and simmer for 5 minutes. Pour half into another pan.

2. Add sweet potatoes and palm fruits to one pan and simmer until sweet potatoes are almost soft. Add diced fruits and simmer 2 more minutes.

3. Add coconut cream and mix well. Bring back to a boil, then lower heat and simmer 1 more minute. Finish cooking sauce by adding lime juice. Cool to room temperature.

4. Prepare rice flour dumplings. Place glutinous rice flour, tapioca flour and salt into a deep mixing bowl. Gradually add water and mix well. Knead into smooth dough. The dough should be soft and elastic. Roll dough into small dumplings; approximately 0.75-cm in diameter, which you directly drop into the pan with simmering palm sugar syrup. This process should only take about 5 minutes until all dough is used up. Once all the dumplings are in the sauce, continue to simmer for 3 more minutes. The starch of the dumplings will lightly thicken the sauce to the right consistency. Allow dumplings to remain in sauce and cool to room temperature.

5. Combine dumplings and fruits and mix well.

6. Serve this delicious, refreshing fruit cocktail at room temperature or chilled with ice.

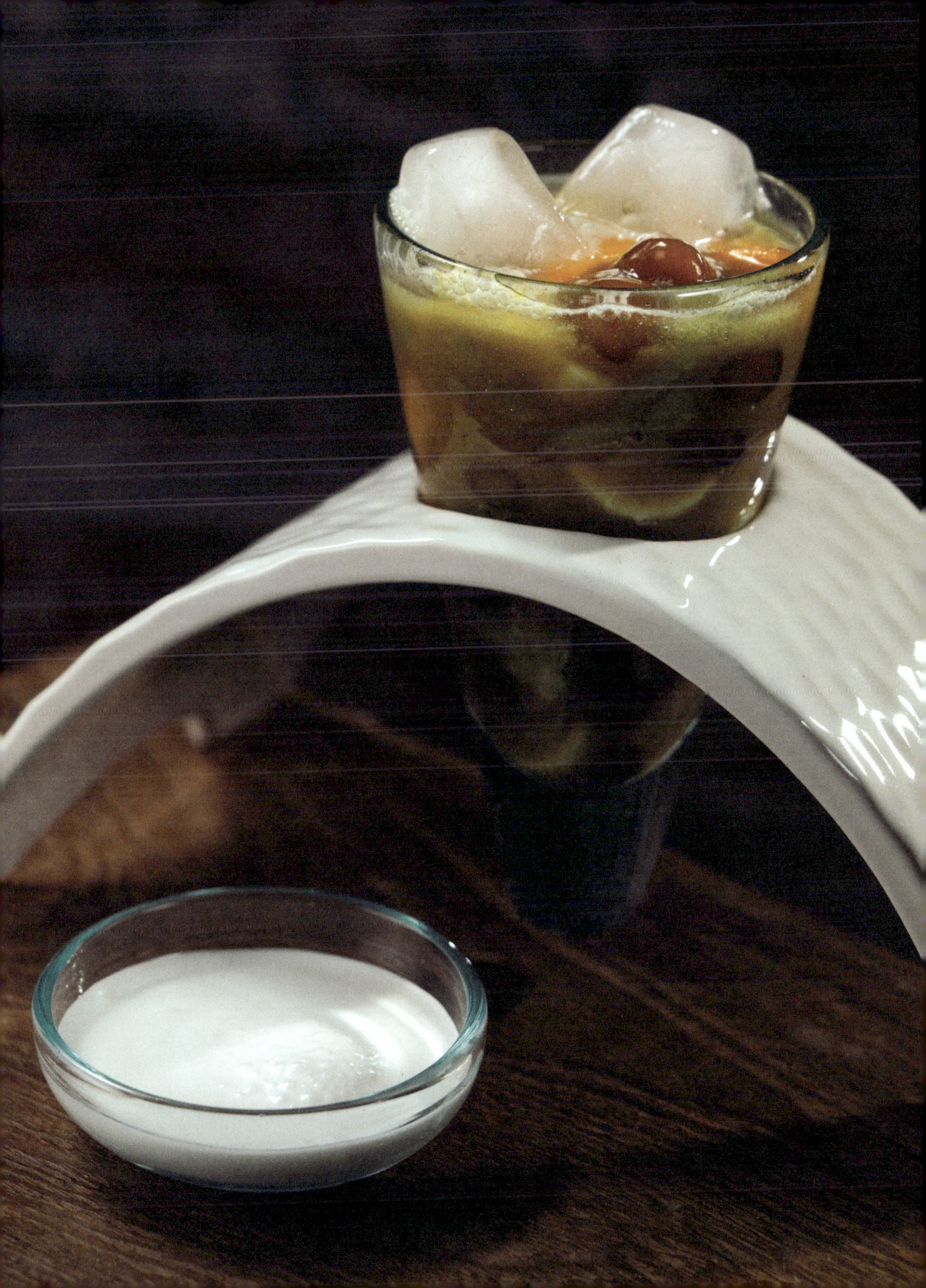

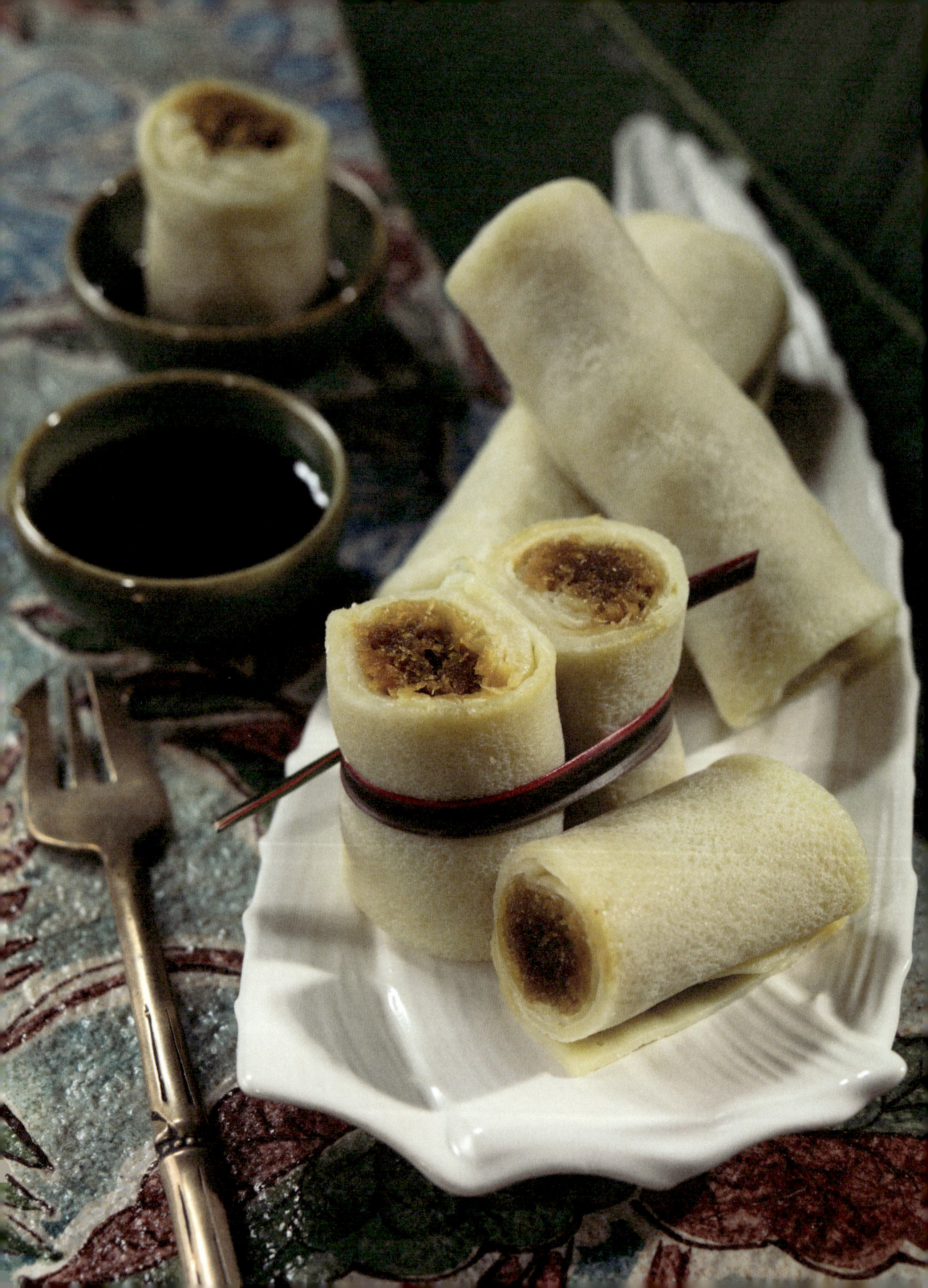

Dadar (Coconut Pancake) Makes about 18 small pieces

These pancakes with a sweet tasty coconut filling known as *unti* are a popular snack. They are often eaten for breakfast together with a piping hot black coffee. Add a scoop of your favourite home-made ice cream and you create an addictive dessert.

PANCAKES
150 g wheat flour, sifted
15 g tapioca flour, sifted
1 egg
15 ml coconut cream
250 ml water
salt, to taste
30 ml vegetable or coconut oil

COCONUT FILLING
75 g palm sugar, grated
90 ml water
salt, to taste
1 pandan leaf, bruised
125 g freshly grated coconut

1. Prepare pancakes. Combine wheat flour, tapioca flour, egg, coconut cream, water, salt and oil in a deep mixing bowl. Stir well with a whisk until no longer lumpy. Strain mixture through a strainer. Batter must be very liquid in consistency.

2. Heat oil in a non-stick pan over low heat. Add 60 ml of batter and cook into a very thin pancake. Repeat until batter is used up. Cool pancakes to room temperature.

3. Prepare filling. Combine palm sugar, water, salt and pandan leaf in saucepan and bring to a boil. Simmer for 3 minutes. Add grated coconut and mix well over low heat for 2 minutes. Cool to room temperature.

4. Place 1 tablespoon of coconut filling on pancake. Fold opposite edges of the pancake together to enclose filling, then roll up tightly.

5. Repeat until all ingredients are used up. Serve warm.

Jaja Sumping Nangka (Steamed Jackfruit Cake)

Makes about 18 small pieces

Basically, the word jaja refers to any kind of snack that is not eaten as a regular meal. At events such as weddings, jaja is the dessert of choice. Jaja is usually enjoyed with a glass of tea or coffee.

180 g rice flour
80 g sugar
500 ml coconut milk
1 pinch salt
12 banana leaf squares, each 15-cm
12 jackfruit segments, halved

1. Combine rice flour, sugar, coconut milk and salt in a non-stick pan and mix well until no longer lumpy.

2. Bring mixture to a gentle boil, then simmer until mixture thickens, whisking constantly to ensure mixture is smooth and free of lumps. Set aside to cool.

3. Place one heaped tablespoon of mixture onto a banana leaf square. Top with a slice of jackfruit and cover with another tablespoon of mixture. Fold two opposite sides of leaf over mixture to enclose, then tuck open ends under parcel. Repeat with remaining ingredients.

4. Steam parcels for about 20 minutes. Serve at room temperature.

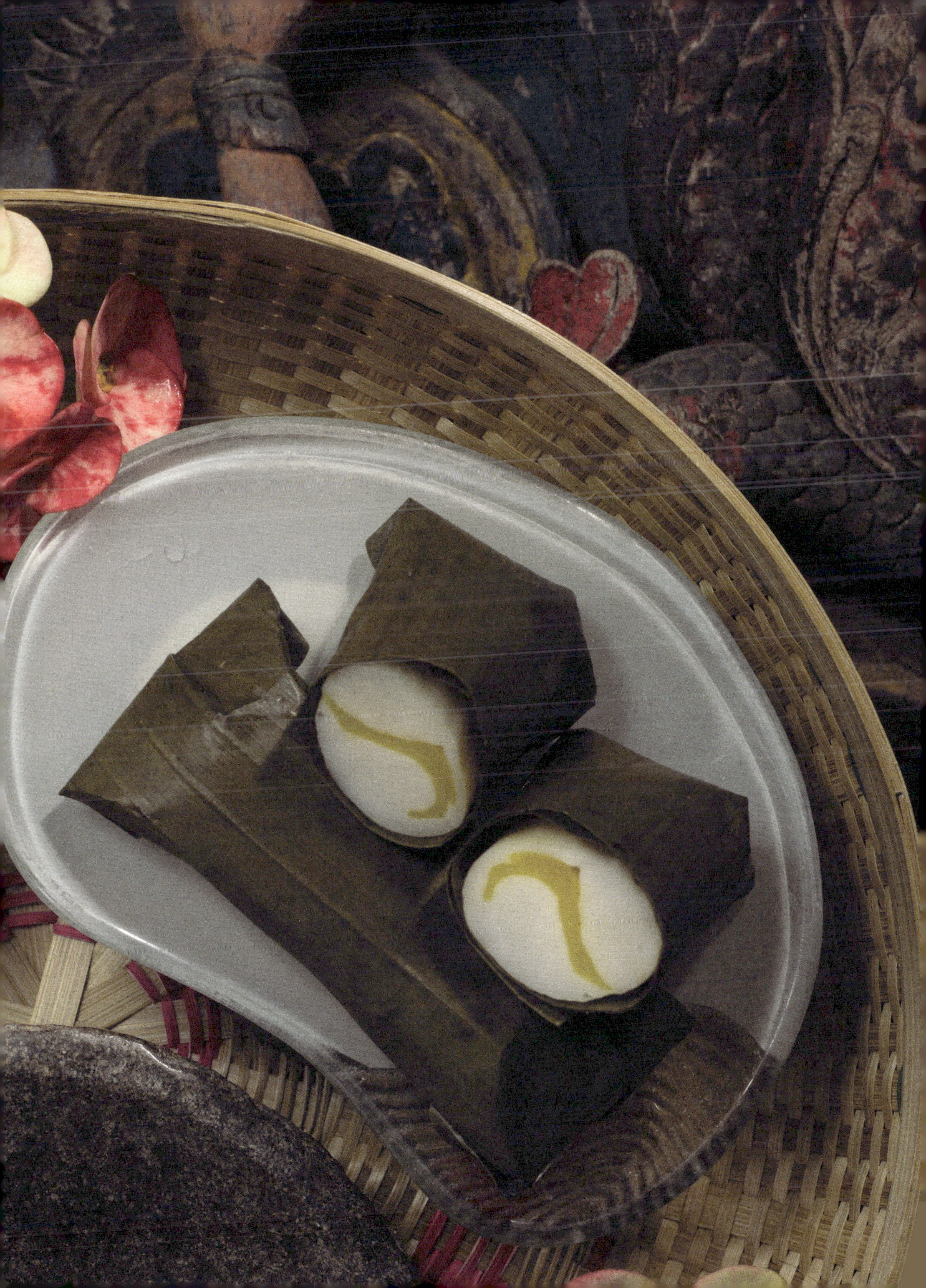

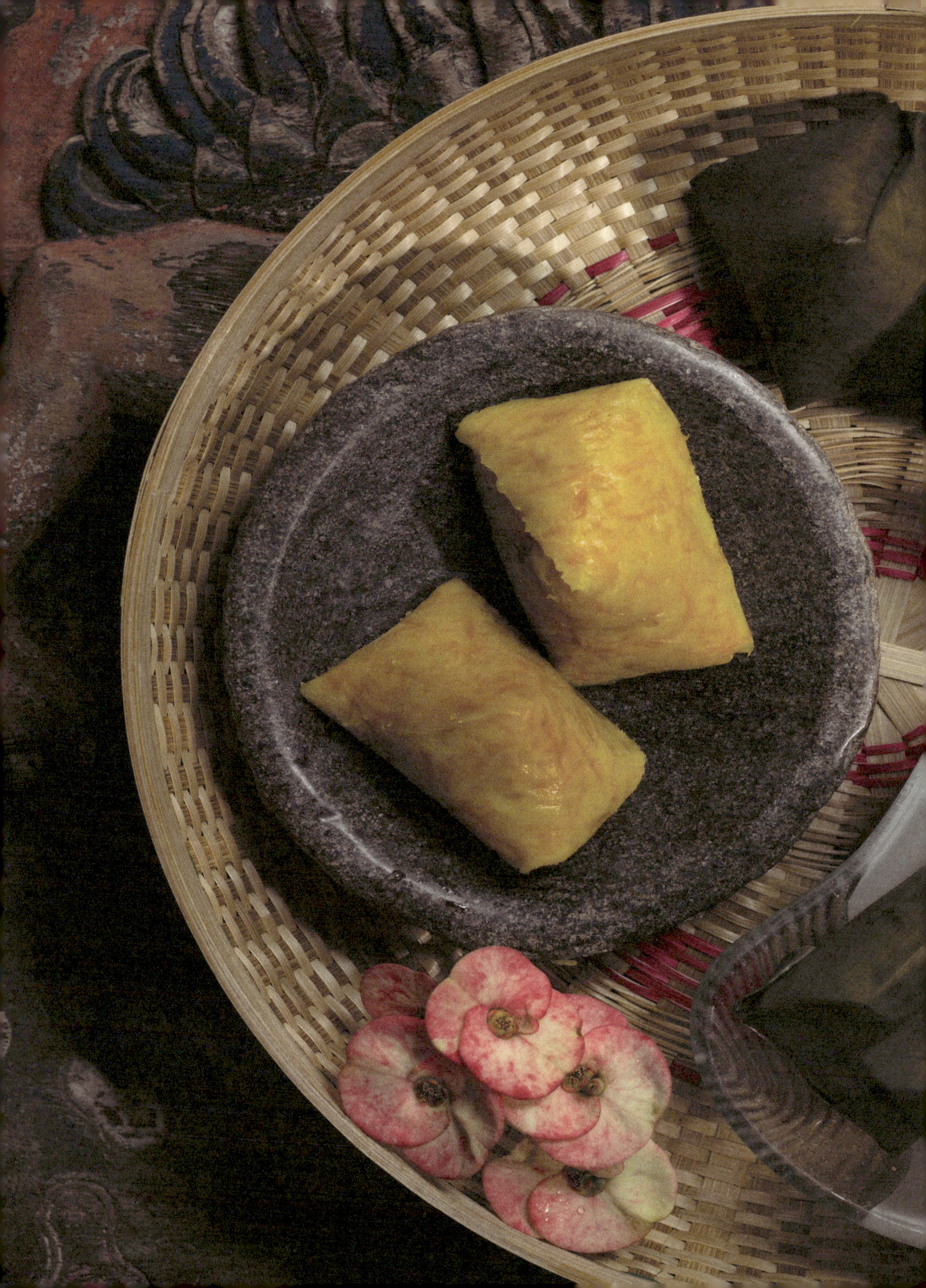

Sumping Waluh (Steamed Pumpkin Cake) Serves 6

The banana leaf is the original disposable, plate and wrapper of Indonesia and all of Asia. There are specific ways in which banana leaves are folded for purposes, and, of course, a specific vocabulary used in connection with each shape. A cake that is wrapped in one way has an entirely different name if it is wrapped in another way. Each type of food must be wrapped in an appropriate manner.

500 g pumpkin, peeled and finely shredded
250 g coconut, freshly shredded
150 g rice flour
100 g crystal (rock) sugar
1 pinch salt
banana leaves, for wrapping
bamboo skewers or toothpicks, as needed
coconut cream, as needed

1. Combine pumpkin, shredded coconut, rice flour, sugar and salt. Mix well.

2. Cut banana leaves into 18 x 22-cm rectangular squares. Steam leaves for 10 seconds or place them for 5 seconds over an open gas flame, or microwave for 3 seconds. This will soften leaf fibres and make banana leaves pliable.

3. Place 2 heaped tablespoons of pumpkin filling on the centre of each banana leaf. Fold one-third of banana leaf over the filling and roll up tightly. Secure ends with bamboo skewers or toothpicks.

4. Steam parcels for 15 minutes.

5. Serve warm and topped with coconut cream.

Glossary

BLACK GLUTINOUS RICE
Black glutinous rice, or sweet black rice is unpolished glutinous rice. In Indonesia, it is commonly used for making cakes and puddings served with palm sugar and coconut cream. The short, round grains are black on the outside but white in the centre.

CANDLENUTS

CANDLENUTS
This is a brittle waxy cream-coloured nut that is similar in appearance to the macadamia nut. It is used as a binding agent and adds a faint flavour to dishes. If not available, use shelled and skinned raw peanuts.

CARDAMOM
The strong, eucalyptus-like flavour of cardamom is not widely used in Balinese cooking except in some chicken and lamb dishes. The cream coloured, fibrous pod encloses pungent black seeds, which release a very strong perfumed aroma when finely crushed in a stone mortar.

CHILLIES

CHILLIES
The Balinese love using chilli in their food and often use an excessive amount. Three types of chillies are used and the level of heat increases as the size decreases. Always wear gloves when handling chillies and wash hands and all surfaces in contact with the chillies thoroughly thereafter as they contain volatile oils that can leave a burning sensation on skin.

LARGE RED CHILLIES
These finger-sized chillies are by far the mildest chillies found in Bali. They are mainly used for flavouring and are always seeded before use. Most recipes in this book make use of these chillies. If the chillies you use are hot, reduce the quantity by one-third.

SMALL CHILLIES
This short, fat chilli is only about 2.5 cm long and it is the most favoured and commonly used chilli in Indonesian cooking. They are normally chopped or bruised before use, adding a good spicy kick to the dishes prepared.

BIRD'S EYE CHILLIES
These tiny green chillies are the spiciest ones. They are mostly used raw to spice up condiments.

CLOVES

CLOVE
The clove tree is a member of the myrtle family and is native to South East Asia. The central mountain ranges of Bali are full of clove trees, easily recognisable from their pretty red flower buds which are dried to make the spice. When dried, the flower buds turn a reddish-brown colour and becomes one of the strongest smelling spices in the world.

COCONUT OIL
This is the preferred oil in Balinese cooking. Coconut oil is now commercially produced. It is cholesterol-free and very

102

light. Substitute with a light vegetable, peanut, sunflower or soy bean oil if unavailable. Sesame and olive oil, are not good substitutes due to their strong flavours.

CORIANDER SEEDS
Coriander seeds are among only a handful of dry spices that are used in Indonesian cooking. The dried seeds are often roasted before being crushed to release their flavour which is delicate yet complex, with a hint of pepper, mint and lemon.

CUMIN

CUMIN
Cumin was highly prized in ancient civilisations as one of the most aromatic of all culinary spices. In Indonesia, cumin has been cultivated for centuries in the mountainous regions and is popularly used in many dishes. Because of its strong flavour, only small quantities are needed to impact the taste of a dish.

GALANGAL

GALANGAL
A relative of the more common ginger, galangal is a standard ingredient in Balinese cooking. It is known as *laos* in Indonesia and greater galangal in English. Young galangal is cream coloured with pink shoots and takes on a darker hue as it ages. Like ginger, its flavour is sharp and spicy but with a sweet citrus-like aroma.

GARLIC
The garlic used in Bali is similar to the common garlic but its cloves are usually smaller with a less pungent flavour.

GINGER
The rhizome of an attractive flowering plant, ginger is widely used in Balinese cooking. Select roots that are plump and firm. Peel then either slice or pound before using. It is easily available in Asian stores and should never be substituted with ground ginger.

KAFFIR LIMES

KAFFIR LIMES
These small green citrus fruit are often used in small quantities in Balinese cooking. The fruit has a marked protrusion on one end and its skin is knobbly and wrinkled. Its taste ranges from sour to bitter and the Balinese prefer it to any other type of lime but the common green lime makes an acceptable substitute.

KAFFIR LIME LEAF

KAFFIR LIME LEAF
The dark green and glossy kaffir lime leaf looks like two leaves joined end to end. Like the kaffir lime, the leaves have a sweet, lemon flavour and can be bruised and added whole to soups and sauces or finely shredded for dry dishes.

LEMON BASIL

Sweet basil is known to have been cultivated in India for 5,000 years. Today it occurs naturally or in naturalised forms throughout the tropics, subtropics and warm temperate areas. Records of its cultivation were found in Egypt 3,000 years ago and it most probably made its way from there to the Middle East, Greece, Italy, and the rest of Europe. This delicate spice has a very pleasant lemon-basil flavour used mostly in fish dishes, which are wrapped in banana leaves before cooking. If used in cooked dishes, then finely sliced lemon basil should be added near the end of the cooking process to retain its clean, lemony fragrance. Regular basil or Thai basil can be used as a substitute for lemon basil.

LESSER GALANGAL

LESSER GALANGAL

Botanically a member of the ginger family, this ingredient is subject to some confusion caused by the many names by which it is known. The Balinese call it "*cekuh*"; for the sake of simplicity we refer to it by its Indonesian name of "*kencur*". *Kencur* is a delicate root with thin brown skin, lemon-coloured crisp flesh, with a unique, very strong, camphor-like, musky, peppery, earthy taste somewhat similar to young ginger and galangal. It has strong, overpowering aroma and must be used sparingly. Of all the spices used in Indonesian cooking, this is one of the most difficult to find in the West. If unavailable, replace a given quantity in a recipe with equal amounts of ginger and galangal.

NUTMEG

NUTMEG

Inside the apricot-like fruit lies a hard seed, the kernel of which is the nutmeg. Around this seed is a lace covering or aril – the by-product of mace. Nutmeg has a rich, fresh and highly aromatic flavour with a hint of clove. Nutmeg is best bought whole and will keep in airtight containers for a long time. Avoid using powdered nutmeg as the flavour would not be at its optimum. Always grate whole nutmegs. This aromatic sweet spice is often used with strongly flavoured meats such as pork, duck and lamb.

PALM SUGAR

PALM SUGAR

Among sugar-producing trees, certain tropical palms rank among the most bountiful in their potential harvest. The sugar and lontar palm or the coconut tree can be tapped for up to half the year, yielding 4–6 litres per day. Individual trees can produce between 5 and 40 kg of sugar per year. The sap is collected from the flowering stalks at the top of the tree, or from taps in the trunk, and then boiled down to a thick syrupy mass which is then poured into halved coconut shells or bamboo stems where it is cooled and set to be sold in cylindrical or round cakes.

PANDAN LEAF

The aromatic leaf of a type of almost thornless pandanus, the screwpine leaf is used for flavouring cakes and snacks. The shredded leaf is also a common topping on offering baskets in Bali.

PEPPERCORNS

PEPPERCORNS

In Balinese cooking, black pepper is more popularly used than white pepper. Grind or crush fresh peppercorns, as ground pepper looses its aroma quickly.

PEANUTS
When choosing raw peanuts, look for those with the skin still on. Peanuts are tastier and more flavoursome when they are deep-fried or roasted in their skins. The second best thing is peanuts which are roasted in the shell. These are available from most supermarkets.

PRAWN (SHRIMP) PASTE, DRIED

PRAWN (SHRIMP) PASTE, DRIED
Made by fermenting tiny prawns and then pounding them into a pulp, this pungent paste is available in small packages from Asia markets. Grill or roast without oil before using. Roasted prawn paste can be stored for several months in an airtight container. Although pungent, prawn paste adds a pleasant flavour when used in dishes.

SALAM LEAVES

SALAM LEAF
The *salam* leaf is used to flavour soups and stews, and vegetable and meat dishes. Although similar to the bay leaf in use and appearance, they are completely different and should not be used as substitutes for each other.

SHALLOTS

SHALLOTS
The common onion available in Bali is small and red, and just slightly different from shallots sold in other parts of the world. If this type of shallot is not available, replace with red Spanish onions.

SOY SAUCE
Soy sauce may be salty (*asin*) or sweet (*manis*). Both varieties are served at the Balinese table. Salty soy sauce is commonly known outside Bali as light soy sauce.

TAMARIND

TAMARIND
The tamarind seed pod ripens on the tree. It contains a fleshy pulp, which has a very sour taste. The pulp needs to be soaked in warm water for 15 minutes, then strained through a fine sieve. The seed and fibres are then discarded. Only the juice is used. Tamarind is widely available in their pods or compressed, minus pods and seeds.

TURMERIC

TURMERIC
Often misspelled and mispronounced as "tumeric", this herbaceous plant is thought to have originated from India. Turmeric now grows in a naturalised state in the teak forests of East Java. An attractive perennial with large lily-like leaves and yellow flowers, turmeric is a member of the ginger family and, like ginger, the underground rhizome stem of the plant is used in cooking. The brownish skin must be scraped or peeled to expose its bright yellow flesh. Fresh turmeric is crunchy with a rich, gingery, citrus aroma and a pleasant earthy flavour. Fresh turmeric adds a wonderful flavour and a rich golden-yellow hue to dishes. If fresh turmeric is not available, substitute with $1^1/_2$ tablespoons turmeric powder per 100 g fresh, peeled roots. In many parts of Indonesia, finely sliced turmeric leaves are used as seasoning in many dishes.

Weights & Measures

Quantities for this book are given in Metric and American (spoon and cup) measures. Standard spoon and cup measurements used are: 1 teaspoon = 5 ml, 1 tablespoon = 15 ml, 1 cup = 250 ml. All measures are level unless otherwise stated.

LIQUID AND VOLUME MEASURES

Metric	Imperial	American
5 ml	1/6 fl oz	1 teaspoon
10 ml	1/3 fl oz	1 dessertspoon
15 ml	1/2 fl oz	1 tablespoon
60 ml	2 fl oz	1/4 cup (4 tablespoons)
85 ml	2 1/2 fl oz	1/3 cup
90 ml	3 fl oz	3/8 cup (6 tablespoons)
125 ml	4 fl oz	1/2 cup
180 ml	6 fl oz	3/4 cup
250 ml	8 fl oz	1 cup
300 ml	10 fl oz (1/2 pint)	1 1/4 cups
375 ml	12 fl oz	1 1/2 cups
435 ml	14 fl oz	1 3/4 cups
500 ml	16 fl oz	2 cups
625 ml	20 fl oz (1 pint)	2 1/2 cups
750 ml	24 fl oz (1 1/5 pints)	3 cups
1 litre	32 fl oz (1 3/5 pints)	4 cups
1.25 litres	40 fl oz (2 pints)	5 cups
1.5 litres	48 fl oz (2 2/5 pints)	6 cups
2.5 litres	80 fl oz (4 pints)	10 cups

DRY MEASURES

Metric	Imperial
30 grams	1 ounce
45 grams	1 1/2 ounces
55 grams	2 ounces
70 grams	2 1/2 ounces
85 grams	3 ounces
100 grams	3 1/2 ounces
110 grams	4 ounces
125 grams	4 1/2 ounces
140 grams	5 ounces
280 grams	10 ounces
450 grams	16 ounces (1 pound)
500 grams	1 pound, 1 1/2 ounces
700 grams	1 1/2 pounds
800 grams	1 3/4 pounds
1 kilogram	2 pounds, 3 ounces
1.5 kilograms	3 pounds, 4 1/2 ounces
2 kilograms	4 pounds, 6 ounces

OVEN TEMPERATURE

	°C	°F	Gas Regulo
Very slow	120	250	1
Slow	150	300	2
Moderately slow	160	325	3
Moderate	180	350	4
Moderately hot	190/200	370/400	5/6
Hot	210/220	410/440	6/7
Very hot	230	450	8
Super hot	250/290	475/550	9/10

LENGTH

Metric	Imperial
0.5 cm	1/4 inch
1 cm	1/2 inch
1.5 cm	3/4 inch
2.5 cm	1 inch

Chef Heinz von Holzen has spent many years investigating and documenting Balinese cooking that is distinct from its Indonesian cousin. He first realised that Bali lacked a restaurant serving authentic local cuisine during his time with the Grand Hyatt Bali. To fill the culinary gap, he opened his first restaurant, Bumbu Bali. Chef Heinz von Holzen then began conducting cooking classes at his restaurant three times a week. His classes became extremely popular, increasing chef Heinz von Holzen's standing as a master of Balinese cuisine and sealing Bumbu Bali's reputation as an authentic Balinese restaurant internationally.

Today, chef Heinz von Holzen runs two other authentic Balinese restaurants, Warung Sate and Pasar Malam. He has also written several cookbooks on Balinese and Indonesian cooking and pictorial books on Bali and Indonesia.

OTHER TITLES BY HEINZ VON HOLZEN

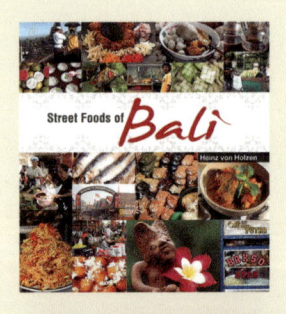

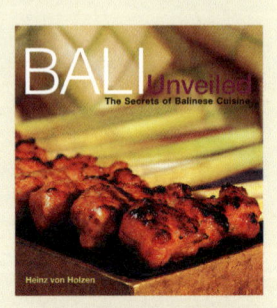